science for a changing world

In cooperation with the National Park Service

Water and Rock Geochemistry, Geologic Cross Sections, Geochemical Modeling, and Groundwater Flow Modeling for Identifying the Source of Groundwater to Montezuma Well, a Natural Spring in Central Arizona

Open-File Report 2011–1063

U.S. Department of Interior
U.S. Geological Survey

Cover: *Left,* Montezuma Well. *Right,* Layered travertine deposit at previous spring source near Montezuma Well.

USGS
science for a changing world

Water and Rock Geochemistry, Geologic Cross Sections, Geochemical Modeling, and Groundwater Flow Modeling for Identifying the Source of Groundwater to Montezuma Well, a Natural Spring in Central Arizona

By Raymond H. Johnson, Ed DeWitt, Laurie Wirt, L. Rick Arnold, and John D. Horton

In cooperation with the National Park Service

Open-File Report 2011–1063

U.S. Department of the Interior
U.S. Geological Survey

U.S. Department of the Interior
KEN SALAZAR, Secretary

U.S. Geological Survey
Marcia K. McNutt, Director

U.S. Geological Survey, Reston, Virginia: 2011

For product and ordering information:
World Wide Web: http://www.usgs.gov/pubprod
Telephone: 1-888-ASK-USGS

For more information on the USGS—the Federal source for science about the Earth,
its natural and living resources, natural hazards, and the environment:
World Wide Web: http://www.usgs.gov
Telephone: 1-888-ASK-USGS

Suggested citation:
Johnson, R.H., DeWitt, Ed, Wirt, Laurie, Arnold, L.R., and Horton, J.D., 2011, Water and rock geochemistry, geologic cross sections, geochemical modeling, and groundwater flow modeling for identifying the source of groundwater to Montezuma Well, a natural spring in central Arizona: U.S. Geological Survey Open-File Report 2011–1063, 62 p.

Any use of trade, product, or firm names is for descriptive purposes only and does not imply
endorsement by the U.S. Government.

Although this report is in the public domain, permission must be secured from the individual
copyright owners to reproduce any copyrighted material contained within this report.

Contents

Problem Statement 1

Research and Report Objectives 1

Physical Setting 2

Data Collection and Sampling Procedures 2

    Water Data 2

    Rock Data 4

Results 5

    Geology and Rock Data 5

    Water Data 6

    Summary Figures for Geochemical Data 6

    Geochemical Modeling 7

    Conceptual Model Summary 9

    Groundwater Modeling 9

        Numerical Simulations 9

        Model Design 9

        Simulation Results 10

            Simulation 1 10

            Simulation 2 10

            Simulation 3 11

            Simulation 4 11

Summary 11

References Cited 11

Figures 14

Appendix 1. Original Water Sample Laboratory Data 62

Appendix 2. Original Rock Sample Laboratory Data 62

Appendix 3. PHREEQC and NETPATH Files 62

Appendix 4. Groundwater Flow Modeling Files 62

Figures

1. Location and details of study area overlain on geologic map with hillshade elevations 14

2. Geologic map with cross-section location and hillshade elevations 15

3. Geologic cross section along A-A' with major rock types 16

4. Aeromagnetic map of Montezuma Well area, Verde Valley 17

5–7. Maps showing—

    5. Location of water samples from 2006 with area of figure 6 outlined 18

    6. Location of water samples from 2006 in immediate Montezuma Well vicinity 19

    7. Location of water samples from 2008 in immediate Montezuma Well vicinity 19

8. Photo of flowing sand "spring" at the "false bottom" of Montezuma Well 20

9. Photo of sampling apparatus with well screen attached to tubing that goes to a peristaltic pump 20

10–12. Maps showing—

    10. Location of rock samples with area of figure 11 outlined 21

    11. Location of rock samples with area of figure 12 outlined 21

12. Location of rock samples in immediate Montezuma Well vicinity. 22

13–15. Graphs showing—
13. Concentrations of iron and calcium in rock samples. 23
14. Concentrations of arsenic and lithium in rock samples. 24
15. Concentrations of strontium and strontium isotopes in rock samples. 25

16. Strontium concentrations and isotopic ratios of major rock types along cross section A-A'. 26
17. Strontium isotopes ratios of major rock types along cross section A-A'. 26
18. Permeabilities of rock units along cross section A-A'. 27
19. Graphs showing oxygen and deuterium isotopes in water samples 29

20–45. Maps showing locations (and concentrations) of—
20. Sample categories and field numbers 30
21. $\delta^{18}O$ in per mil 31
22. δD in per mil 32
23. Specific conductance in µS/cm 33
24. pH 34
25. Temperature in °C 35
26. Dissolved oxygen in mg/L 36
27. Arsenic in µg/L 37
28. Log partial pressure of carbon dioxide 38
29. Chloride in mg/L 39
30. Calcium in mg/L 40
31. Alkalinity as $CaCO_3$ in mg/L 41
32. Cesium in µg/L 42
33. Boron in µg/L 43
34. Lithium in µg/L 44
35. Potassium in mg/L 45
36. Magnesium in mg/L 46
37. Sodium in mg/L 47
38. Sulfate in mg/L 48
39. Silica in mg/L 49
40. Strontium in µg/L 50
41. $^{87}Sr/^{86}Sr$ 51
42. $\delta^{13}C$ ‰ 52
43. ^{14}C as percent modern carbon 53
44. Tritium reported in tritium units 54
45. Calcite saturation index 55

46–49. Graphs showing—
46. Selected constituents normalized to Montezuma Well with upgradient and shallow zones. 56
47. Selected constituents normalized to Montezuma Well with upgradient, mixing, and shallow zones. 57
48. Arsenic and calcium concentrations compared to chloride concentrations for all water samples. 58
49. Silica and strontium concentrations compared to chloride concentrations for all water samples. 59

50. Groundwater flow paths and strontium isotopic ratios in surface waters and wells. 60
51. Hydraulic heads and flow lines with no basalt dike. 60
52. Hydraulic heads and flow lines with basalt dike. 61
53. Hydraulic heads and flow lines with basalt dike and drain. 61

figure files (Figures.zip) .... link

Tables

1. Water sample data .... link
2. Rock sample data .... link
3. Strontium concentrations and isotope data in rock .... link

Appendixes

1. Original Water Sample Laboratory Data.. link
2. Original Rock Sample Laboratory Data .... link
3. PHREEQC and NETPATH Files... link
4. Groundwater Flow Modeling Files .... link

Conversion Factors

Inch/Pound to SI

Multiply	By	To obtain
Length		
inch (in.)	2.54	centimeter (cm)
inch (in.)	25.4	millimeter (mm)
foot (ft)	0.3048	meter (m)
mile (mi)	1.609	kilometer (km)
yard (yd)	0.9144	meter (m)
Volume		
ounce, fluid (fl. oz)	0.02957	liter (L)
pint (pt)	0.4732	liter (L)
quart (qt)	0.9464	liter (L)
gallon (gal)	3.785	liter (L)
gallon (gal)	0.003785	cubic meter (m^3)
cubic inch (in^3)	0.01639	liter (L)
cubic foot (ft^3)	0.02832	cubic meter (m^3)
cubic yard (yd^3)	0.7646	cubic meter (m^3)
Flow rate		
foot per second (ft/s)	0.3048	meter per second (m/s)
cubic foot per second (ft^3/s)	0.02832	cubic meter per second (m^3/s)
Mass		
ounce, avoirdupois (oz)	28.35	gram (g)
pound, avoirdupois (lb)	0.4536	kilogram (kg)
Pressure		
Atmosphere, standard (atm)	101.3	kilopascal (kPa)

Temperature in degrees Fahrenheit (°F) may be converted to degrees Celsius (°C) as follows:
°C=(°F-32)/1.8

Vertical coordinate information is referenced to the North American Vertical Datum of 1929 (NAVD 29).
Horizontal coordinate information is referenced to the North American Datum of 1927 (NAD 27).

SI to Inch/Pound

Multiply	By	To obtain
Length		
centimeter (cm)	0.3937	inch (in.)
millimeter (mm)	0.03937	inch (in.)
meter (m)	3.281	foot (ft)
kilometer (km)	0.6214	mile (mi)
meter (m)	1.094	yard (yd)
Volume		
liter (L)	33.82	ounce, fluid (fl. oz)
liter (L)	2.113	pint (pt)
liter (L)	1.057	quart (qt)
liter (L)	0.2642	gallon (gal)
cubic meter (m^3)	264.2	gallon (gal)
liter (L)	61.02	cubic inch (in^3)
cubic meter (m^3)	35.31	cubic foot (ft^3)
cubic meter (m^3)	1.308	cubic yard (yd^3)
Flow rate		
meter per second (m/s)	3.281	foot per second (ft/s)
cubic meter per second (m^3/s)	35.31	cubic foot per second (ft^3/s)
Mass		
gram (g)	0.03527	ounce, avoirdupois (oz)
kilogram (kg)	2.205	pound avoirdupois (lb)
Pressure		
kilopascal (kPa)	0.009869	atmosphere, standard (atm)

Temperature in degrees Celsius (°C) may be converted to degrees Fahrenheit (°F) as follows:
°F=(1.8×°C)+32
Vertical coordinate information is referenced to the North American Vertical Datum of 1929 (NAVD 29).
Horizontal coordinate information is referenced to the North American Datum of 1927 (NAD 27).

Abbreviations Used in This Report

°C	degrees Celcius
mg/L	milligrams per liter
µg/L	micrograms per liter
µS/cm	microSiemens per centimeter
‰	per mil (or parts per thousand)
$\delta^{18}O$	delta notation for the ration of oxygen-18/oxygen-16, expressed in per mil or parts per thousand
δD	delta notation for the ration of hydrogen-2/hydrogen-1, expressed in per mil or parts per thousand

Water and Rock Geochemistry, Geologic Cross Sections, Geochemical Modeling, and Groundwater Flow Modeling for Identifying the Source of Groundwater to Montezuma Well, a Natural Spring in Central Arizona

By Raymond H. Johnson, Ed DeWitt, Laurie Wirt, L. Rick Arnold, and John D. Horton

Problem Statement

The National Park Service (NPS) seeks additional information to better understand the source(s) of groundwater and associated groundwater flow paths to Montezuma Well (fig. 1) in Montezuma Castle National Monument, central Arizona. The source of water to Montezuma Well, a flowing sinkhole in a desert setting (see picture on cover), is poorly understood. Water emerges from the middle limestone facies of the lacustrine Verde Formation (Twenter and Metzger, 1963), but the precise origin of the water and its travel path are largely unknown (McKee and others, 1947; Lange, 1957). Some have proposed artesian flow to Montezuma Well through the Supai Formation, which is exposed along the eastern margin of the Verde Valley and underlies the Verde Formation (Konieczki and Leake, 1997). The groundwater recharge zone likely lies above the floor of the Verde Valley somewhere to the north or east of Montezuma Well, where precipitation is more abundant. Additional data from groundwater, surface water, and bedrock geology are required for Montezuma Well and the surrounding region to test the current conceptual ideas, to provide new details on the groundwater flow in the area, and to assist in future management decisions. The results of this research will provide information for long-term water resource management and the protection of water rights.

Research and Report Objectives

The first objective is to develop a conceptual hydrogeologic framework model that identifies the principal stratigraphic and structural features that serve as constraints or conduits for groundwater movement for the region surrounding Montezuma Well. This framework will integrate available geologic, geophysical, hydrological, and geochemical data.

The second objective of this research is to identify travel paths for groundwater supplying Montezuma Well and the surrounding region, on the basis of chemical and isotopic analyses of groundwater samples and rock samples. Isotopic and chemical data are being used as naturally-occurring tracers of recharge source areas and water-rock interactions.

The purpose of this Open-File Report (OFR) is to release the groundwater chemistry, rock data, geologic cross sections, and groundwater flow modeling related to completing the above research objectives. Detailed interpretations related to this release will be provided in subsequent journal articles.

Much of the wording in this report has technical details. Several glossaries are available online that cover definitions of technical geologic and hydrologic words. Geologic glossaries are offered online by the U.S. Geological Survey and the National Park Service (*http://www.nature.nps.gov/geology/usgsnps/misc/glossaryAtoC.html*) and by Cengage Learning (*http://college.cengage.com/geology/resources/geologylink/glossary.html*). Hydrologic glossaries are offered online by the U.S. Geological Survey Oregon Water Science Center (*http://or.water.usgs.gov/projs_dir/willgw/glossary.html*) and Georgia Water Science Center (*http://ga.water.usgs.gov/edu/dictionary.html*).

Physical Setting

Montezuma Well is a spring-fed sinkhole on the north bank of Wet Beaver Creek (fig. 1), about 8 miles (mi) northeast of the town of Camp Verde in the Verde Valley of Arizona. Montezuma Well is part of the Montezuma Castle National Monument, managed by the NPS. Wet Beaver Creek is a predominantly gaining stream from its origin at Wet Beaver Creek Spring to below Montezuma Well (fig. 1) and is perennial to a point downstream from Montezuma Castle.

The climate of the study area is arid to semiarid, with a bimodal pattern of precipitation caused by winter storms and summer monsoons. Spatial differences in temperature and precipitation vary greatly and are largely governed by elevation and the season of the year. The Verde Valley basin receives a majority of its recharge from the high-altitude rim region to the north and east (Twenter and Metzger, 1963, p. 67).

The Verde Valley is the transition zone between the Colorado Plateau, which forms the high-altitude rim to the north and east (Mogollon Rim), and the Basin and Range province. In this area, the Colorado Plateau is extensively covered by basalt flows. The Verde Formation is a limestone deposit formed during regional extension approximately 5–10 million years ago. The geology mapped by Weir and others (1989) is presented in figure 2, which includes the location of a geologic cross section. This cross section (fig. 3) was created specifically for this research and is based on available well logs, the mapped geology, and geophysical interpretations. Figure 4 shows the geophysical details from an aeromagnetic map of the area with explanations of the interpretations that were used to help create the geologic cross section. The extension and downward faulting in the area is immediately apparent by following the elevation of the Permian Sandstones or any other unit that forms the geology in the Colorado Plateau (fig. 3). A summary of the geologic history of the area can be found in Ranney (2001). The geologic history of the area is important in understanding how the current geology was formed. However, the focus of this report is a detailed description of the subsurface geology in order to understand water-rock interactions. The geochemistry of these interactions assists in identifying groundwater flow paths and sources of groundwater to Montezuma Well.

Data Collection and Sampling Procedures

Water Data

Spring, well, and stream water samples were collected in the area around Montezuma Well at the locations in figures 5, 6, and 7. Sampling was completed in three rounds: May 2006, October 2006, and April 2008. Water sample locations and data maps throughout this report have been split according to year. Water sample locations from 2006 are presented in figures 5 and 6, and water sample locations from 2008 are presented in figure 7. The April 2008 sampling round was completed in order to provide repeat sampling at many locations, add some additional shallow well sampling, provide for improved alkalinity measurements (discussed below), and provide for the collection of additional helium isotope data (which will be released and discussed in a subsequent journal article). All water data, along with sample type (that is, spring, well, or stream), are included in table 1. All original laboratory data and field parameters including pH, water temperature, specific conductance, alkalinity, and dissolved oxygen are provided in appendix 1. Water samples were collected either through tubing connected to a peristaltic pump or with a plastic syringe. Larger, more accessible springs were sampled using a peristaltic pump, where the sample tubing was placed to the desired depth. Shallow, less accessible springs were sampled using a plastic syringe. Wells were sampled using the peristaltic pump with pumped well water constantly flowing through a clean, plastic collection bottle. Any available well information (well identification, depth, etc.) is provided in table 1. All samples were field filtered. The peristaltic pump samples used an in-line 0.45–micrometer (µm) capsule filter and syringe samples used a syringe-mounted 0.45-µm disc filter.

Montezuma Well has a "false bottom" with two main springs of "flowing sand" (Konieczki and Leake, 1997) which are referred to as the East and West vents, based on location. In the area of these two main springs, the hard bottom occurs at a depth of approximately 55 feet (ft) below the water's surface, and the "false bottom" refers to the visible top of the flowing sands in the spring vents (fig. 8), which also occurs at approximately 55 ft. Groundwater samples were collected at depth within these two springs of flowing sand. The exact shape and depth of these spring vents are unknown. Sampling was achieved using a small well screen (1-inch [in] diameter with 0.010-in slots) connected to polyethylene tubing (1/4-in) that was connected to the peristaltic pump at the water's surface (fig. 9). The deepest sample collected was at 130 ft below the water's surface in the East vent. In 2006, divers assisted in the placement of the sampling apparatus, which included added weights to overcome the upward force of the flowing sands and a YSI HydroLab that measured field parameters at depth (shown going into the sand in fig. 8 and attached to apparatus in fig. 9). Note that for specific conductance measurements, the YSI HydroLab was measuring water and flowing sand as a bulk measurement, thus making the reported measurements in the Montezuma Well vents low because of the highly resistive sand. In 2008, the same sampling apparatus was used again to sample the same main springs. During this round, divers were not used and the sampling personnel were able to locate the main springs by tapping the bottom until the apparatus was able to go to a depth greater than 55 ft. Placement of the apparatus into the spring vent was confirmed by removing the peristaltic pump and checking that the spring water flowed through the tubing under artesian pressure. This flow did not occur if the apparatus was not truly in a spring vent. The YSI HydroLab was not used in the 2008 sampling; instead, all field parameters were measured directly on the flowing water at the surface, which did not include any flowing sand.

Ten aliquots of water provided samples for (1) strontium isotopes, (2) sulfur isotopes, (3) carbon isotopes, (4) tritium, (5) isotopes of oxygen and hydrogen, (6) dissolved major and minor cations and sulfate, (7) dissolved major cations only, (8) dissolved major anions, (9) alkalinity, and (10) arsenic concentrations and speciation. All original laboratory data can be found in appendix 1. Water samples for inductively coupled plasma–mass spectrometry (ICP-MS) and inductively coupled plasma–atomic emission spectrometry (ICP-AES) analyses were acidified to a pH<2 with ultrapure nitric acid. Water samples for ion chromatography (IC) and alkalinity were refrigerated for preservation. Alkalinity was determined by automatic titration ("Mineral's Lab" column in table 1) and manual titration ("Johnson titration" column in table 1) to a pH of 4.5. However, degassing of carbon dioxide (CO_2) in these samples created calcite precipitation that did not fully dissolve during alkalinity measurements. For the 2006 samples, alkalinity was also determined through geochemical modeling (PHREEQC, Parkhurst and Appelo, 1999) using alkalinity as a charge balance component ("PHREEQC calculated" column in table 1). For the 2008 samples, alkalinity was measured immediately in the field in order to minimize CO_2 degassing. The majority of strontium and all sulfur isotopic analyses were completed by the USGS Mineral Resources Laboratory (Denver, Colo.) on a Nu Plasma multi-collector–inductively coupled plasma–mass spectrometer (MC-ICP-MS) using a desolvating nebulizer. Five strontium isotope samples were analyzed at the University of Colorado– Geosciences Department Laboratory using thermal ionization mass spectrometry (TIMS). Only selected samples were collected for tritium and carbon isotopes, which were analyzed by the Laboratory of Isotope Geochemistry at the University of Arizona in Tucson, Ariz. Carbon isotopes were analyzed using an accelerated mass spectrometer (AMS; see *http://www.physics.arizona.edu/ams/education/ams_principle.htm* for the basic principles of AMS), and tritium was measured using liquid scintillation counting. The 2008 tritium analyses were completed by the USGS Noble Gas Laboratory in Denver, Colo., using the helium in-growth method (Bayer and others, 1989; Clark and Fritz, 1997; Demange and others, 2002). With this method, the tritium is allowed to decay and produce the helium-3 (^{3}He) isotope, which is subsequently measured on a mass spectrometer. The total "in-growth" of ^{3}He is used to calculate the amount of tritium present in the sample. This method was used because it has a low detection limit (0.01 tritium units). The oxygen and hydrogen isotopic compositions of water (δ^{18}O, δD) were performed by the USGS Crustal Imaging Team Laboratory in Denver, Colo. Oxygen isotopic compositions were determined using a Micromass Optima, with an automated CO_2 equilibration technique adapted from Epstein and Mayeda (1953). Water samples were prepared for hydrogen-isotopic analyses using the zinc-reduction technique (Kendall and Coplen, 1985). The hydrogen analyses were preformed on a Finnigan MAT 252 mass spectrometer. Values of δ^{18}O and δD are relative to VSMOW (Vienna Standard Mean Ocean Water) and have a reproducibility of approximately 0.2 and 1.0 per mil, respectively.

Analyses for major and minor cations and anions were completed at the USGS Mineral Resources Laboratory (Denver, Colo.). Major and minor cations plus sulfate were completed using ICP-MS (Lamothe and others, 2002) and ICP-AES (Briggs, 2002a). Anion analyses were completed using IC (Theodorakos and others, 2002). Measurements of alkalinity were completed at the USGS Mineral Resources Laboratory (Denver, Colo.) using an automated titrator and separately using manual incremental titration, both to a pH of 4.5. Because of CO_2 degassing, calcite precipitation, and alkalinity reported in a field blank, the lab alkalinity data from 2006 are not deemed reliable. Reproducibility of the ICP-MS and ICP-AES data are generally within 5 percent, and three field blanks were collected to identify contamination during sampling (no significant contamination was found). Total arsenic and arsenic species concentrations (designated as Breit in table 1) were measured using atomic fluorescence spectrometry (AFS) (Corns and others, 1993). Arsenic species were measured by passing the water sample through an anion exchange column with a phosphate mobile phase prior to AFS analysis (Moreno and others, 2000). Both methods were calibrated using freshly prepared standards, and errors were within 5 percent for total and speciation analyses.

Rock Data

Rock samples were collected in the area around Montezuma Well at the locations shown in figures 10, 11, and 12 (formation names are included for reference) in October 2006. Rock samples were prepared by crushing and grinding then dry sieving to less than 150 microns (Taylor and Theodorakos, 2002). The prepared sample was then digested using multiple acids (Briggs and Meier, 2002; Briggs, 2002b) (thus the reference to this procedure as "whole-rock" analysis) and then analyzed for major and trace elements plus boron and strontium isotopes (^{87}Sr/^{86}Sr). All 2006 rock data are reported in table 2 and all original laboratory data is provided in appendix 2. The ICP-MS analyses (Briggs and Meier, 2002) were performed by the USGS Mineral Resources analytical laboratories in Denver, Colo., and the ICP-AES analyses (Briggs, 2002b) were completed on a sample splits by SGS Minerals in Toronto, Ontario, Canada. Both laboratories use the same multiple acid digestion method to completely dissolve the solid material, and elemental data are reported in parts per million (ppm) or as a percentage of the solid-phase total. The strontium isotopes ($^{87}Sr/^{86}Sr$) on rock samples were determined using the same acid digest method and analyzed on a Nu plasma MC-ICP-MS using a desolvating nebulizer.

Results

All of the results provided in this section are intended to release and summarize all of the collected data. Interpretation of these data will be provided in subsequent journal articles.

Geology and Rock Data

The detailed geologic units of the area are shown in figures 2 and 3, including all formation names and well log locations. The geology and whole-rock data can be summarized more easily by grouping the various rock formations. For the whole-rock data (table 2), the rock samples are grouped as travertine, Verde limestone, other Verde samples, basalt, and upgradient samples (these same groupings are given in table 2). The travertine deposits occur only in the immediate Montezuma Well vicinity (fig. 3) and are mapped in more detail by Donchin (1983). The Verde limestone is very heterogeneous, and samples that were not pure limestone were included in a separate group (other Verde samples). These samples included evaporites, red clayey and (or) silty limestone, and basalt conglomerates within the Verde limestone. All basalt samples are pure basalt and do not include the basalt conglomerate sample within the Verde Formation. The upgradient samples are from the Permian age units (sandstones and limestones), which are upgradient in groundwater flow and elevation from Montezuma Well.

Using these groupings, a series of box and whisker plots (figs. 13–15) show the varying rock compositions. The concentrations of calcium in the travertine and the Verde limestone (fig. 13) approach 500,000 ppm (or 50 percent by weight), indicating rocks that are almost pure calcium carbonate. The other Verde samples have much less total calcium and larger amounts of iron (fig. 13), with oxidized and precipitated iron often giving the rock a reddish color. Large iron concentrations uniquely identify the basalts (fig. 13). The upgradient rocks (fig. 13) are sandstones that are mostly pure quartz and have low calcium and iron concentrations, as expected. Overall, each rock type is well identified by simply looking at the iron and calcium concentrations. In addition, arsenic and lithium appear to be uniquely high in the other Verde samples (fig. 14), most likely due to adsorption on iron and (or) clay minerals. Arsenic is also slightly elevated in the travertine samples (fig. 14).

The use of strontium concentrations and isotope ratios in rocks and water in the area around Montezuma Well was a basis for this research. Previous data (table 3) indicated that the basalts have high strontium concentrations, yet the strontium isotope ratios ($^{87}Sr/^{86}Sr$) are low; the opposite is seen in the Permian Sandstones. Given this knowledge, samples for strontium concentrations and isotope ratios of the rock and the water should be good indicators of the groundwater flow paths. Data for this report indicate strontium concentrations are distinctly elevated in the basalt samples and the other Verde samples (fig. 15 and table 3). Much of the elevated concentrations of strontium in the other Verde group are found in the evaporite deposits. The strontium isotope ratios are distinctly low in the basalt samples and high in the upgradient group (fig. 15 and table 3), as expected.

The previous cross section (A-A', fig. 3) is presented again with the strontium concentrations and isotopic ratios plotted for the major rock types (fig. 16); a simplified version with just the strontium isotopic concentrations is also provided (fig. 17). The key point for the strontium data is the high strontium concentrations and low isotopic ratios for the basalts (fuschia color in fig. 16) compared to the low strontium concentrations and high isotopic ratios for the Permian sandstones and shales (brown color in fig. 16). The Paleozoic limestones and the Verde Formation are both low in strontium concentration and intermediate in strontium isotopic ratio. Data for the basement granitic rocks (table 3) show much higher strontium isotope ratios than any sedimentary rock in the area.

In order to evaluate possible groundwater flow paths, the geologic units were also grouped according to permeability (fig. 18) based on rock type. In general, the highest permeability rocks are the horizontal basalts and the Paleozoic limestones (especially the Redwall Limestone). Intermediate permeability formations include the Paleozoic clastic sedimentary rocks and the Verde Formation (decreased permeability due to silts and clays). The lowest permeability rocks are the granitic basement and the vertical basalt dikes. The basalt dikes are inferred to be of low permeability due to slower cooling rates and less fracturing, although the surrounding rocks might be highly fractured, causing the permeability to be higher than otherwise expected.

Water Data

All water sample locations are shown on figures 5, 6, and 7 with data provided in table 1. A graph of all $\delta^{18}O$ and δD isotope samples in water is provided in figures 19A (2006 samples), 19B (2008 samples), and 19C (both years). Figures 20A (2006 samples) and 20B (2008 samples) provide an interpretation of water sources as upgradient, deep, shallow, or mixed, which is discussed briefly in the next paragraph. A series of maps with the geochemical water data are given in figures 21–45; for each of these figures, part A shows data for 2006 samples and part B shows data for 2008 samples. For 2006 samples (figs. 21–45), because several samples were taken at Montezuma Well, Soda Springs, and Montezuma Haven, only the following samples are plotted on the map: MOWE-East-80, SODA-1, and Mont. Haven #3. For 2008 samples, Montezuma Well is plotted for MOWE-East data only and Soda Springs is plotted for SODA-A data only. In addition, for 2008 samples WB-LMBridge and LMBridge-Seep, the sample locations are so close together that the plotted points overlap and appear as only one point, so sample values for WB-LMBridge (stream) are plotted closest to the point and values for LMBridge-Seep (groundwater) are second farthest from the point.

In figures 21–45 and table 1, water samples are grouped into upgradient, shallow, deep, and mixing zones in order to clearly identify differing water types. These groupings are based on location and the subsequent geochemistry. Upgradient samples are any water samples collected outside of the Verde Formation (table 1 and blue sample locations in fig. 20) and include upgradient stream water samples. The shallow samples (table 1 and yellow samples in fig. 20) are within the Verde Formation but have different geochemistry than deep water samples, especially lower chloride values. Groundwater samples from Soda Springs and Montezuma Well are considered deep groundwater sources (table 1 and red samples in fig. 20) because their geochemistry is unique with high concentrations of carbon dioxide, calcium, chloride, arsenic, and other elements. The groundwater samples that are farther downgradient from Montezuma Well are considered to occur in an area of possible groundwater mixing within the Verde Formation (table 1 and orange samples in fig. 20). These samples have geochemistry that is similar to the deeper groundwater, yet they are lower in carbon dioxide, arsenic, and chloride concentrations. Two stream water samples at the Lake Montezuma Bridge are classified as mixing zone samples, as they are downgradient from Montezuma Well and Soda Springs discharge in Wet Beaver Creek. These sample categories and their interpretations relating to groundwater sources to Montezuma Well will be discussed in more detail in subsequent journal articles.

Summary Figures for Geochemical Data

Figures 46 and 47 were created to allow for easier comparison of each groundwater category designation. These figures use only data from the 2006 samples because the upgradient category dataset is more complete. Figure 46 presents the upgradient and shallow categories, and figure 47 adds the mixing category for comparison. The upgradient category data (figs. 46 and 47) is the average value for all the upgradient samples listed in table 1 (2006 data only). Because the deep groundwater category has data with a distinct trend, only the MOWE-East-80 sample was plotted in figures 46 and 47; this is the "reference" sample that the other samples are normalized against. Given the limited samples for the other categories, the mixing category uses only Mont. Haven #3 and the shallow category uses only MOWE-Residence. In figures 46 and 47, each sample value is divided by the MOWE-East-80 sample to provide a normalized value for each constituent presented.

Trend lines for all 2006 data comparing chloride to arsenic and chloride to calcium are presented in figure 48. Arsenic and calcium both appear to correlate quite well with chloride concentrations. Similarly, trend lines for all 2006 data comparing chloride to silica and strontium are presented in figure 49. Silica and strontium do not show any apparent correlations.

Geochemical Modeling

Geochemical modeling to calculate mineral saturation indices was completed on all water samples using PHREEQC (Parkhurst and Appelo, 1999); these results are included in appendix 3. The saturation indices for calcite, dolomite, barite, and chalcedony are also included in table 1. A saturation index less than zero indicates possible mineral dissolution and an index greater than zero indicates possible mineral precipitation (given the analytical data for that water sample). Calcite saturation indices are plotted in figure 45. These data show that calcite may be slightly undersaturated in the upgradient waters (Lodge sample saturation index = -1.34) and is supersaturated in the downgradient stream sample (saturation index = 1.10, due to excess carbon dioxide being degassed and creating calcite precipitation).

Inverse geochemical modeling goes beyond simple saturation index calculations by using a mass balance approach. The generation of a "final" water from an "initial" water (in terms of geochemistry) given the mass of constituents in solution are adjusted through the dissolution or precipitation of assumed mineral phases (Parkhurst and Appelo, 1999). Uncertainty in this procedure occurs from analytical errors, incorrect assumptions of the appropriate mineral phases, and the fact that multiple models may produce the same mass balance (many different minerals can produce the same dissolved constituents). However, the carbonate system around Montezuma Well is relatively well constrained, and the same suite of minerals provided good inverse models in all cases (appendix 3). Inverse modeling was completed with the Lodge well as the initial water (recharge water) and various final waters. The results (appendix 3) are typical of a carbonate system with the dissolution of calcite, dolomite, halite, and gypsum, and some cation exchange. Various pairs of initial recharge waters and final discharge waters were tested, but the results were all quite similar. The upgradient waters all have dissolved inorganic carbon concentrations typical of shallow groundwaters that have recharged through the soil zone. These waters then evolve into Montezuma Well-like deep groundwater with large additions of carbon dioxide or into Verde Valley groundwater like the "MOWE-Residence" sample that has reached final carbonate equilibrium with the surrounding formation. For the deep groundwaters, the large addition of carbon dioxide is not typical of a standard carbonate system, but rather is typical of a travertine forming system, where added carbon dioxide at depth enhances carbonate dissolution, which then precipitates travertine (pure calcium carbonate) at the surface as the carbon dioxide degasses (which lowers the calcium carbonate solubility). These reactions are important to include in ^{14}C age dating, as discussed below, which is the reason for completing the inverse modeling. The final inverse models (appendix 3) use only the Lodge sample as the initial water and only samples that have ^{14}C measurements are used for the final waters.

Carbon-13 (^{13}C) isotope analyses were added as an additional constraint in the inverse modeling. Carbon-13 isotopes were measured to provide additional data on the groundwater flow system and associated geochemical reactions. In most natural system, ^{13}C is dissolved into the groundwater as it is recharged through the unsaturated zone. The processes that determine the ^{13}C isotope value is complex but they typically produce a ^{13}C value in the range of -16 to -12 per mil (Appelo and Postma, 2005). Carbon-13 values that are well outside of that range indicate different geochemical processes.

Carbon-14 (^{14}C) is a radioactive isotope of carbon which is constantly produced in the atmosphere and has a half-life of 5,730 years. As a result, the amount of ^{14}C in a groundwater sample can be used as an age-dating tool. However, all carbon sources must be accounted for in the sample (hence the use of inverse modeling) as "dead" carbon such as carbon in calcite (rocks that are millions of years old) does not contain any ^{14}C. Any groundwater that has dissolved additional carbon from sources other than the reactions occurring during recharge must be adjusted appropriately. Carbon-13 and carbon-14 isotopes (figs. 42 and 43, respectively) were measured at several locations to assist with groundwater age dating. Carbon-14 is reported in percent modern carbon (pMC), where modern carbon is carbon derived from the atmosphere.

The ^{13}C values in the recharging groundwater in the area are in the range of -14 to -10 per mil (WBS-1, WB-Ranger, and WCS-1, table 1 and fig. 42). These values are typical for groundwaters where calcite dissolution occurs due to the presence of $CO_2(gas)$ in the soil within the recharge area. However, the waters within the Verde Valley in 2006 were -1.8, -2.0, and -1.1 (fig. 42A) in the MOWE-Residence, MOWE-West-118, and SODA-1 samples, respectively (table 1), with similar values in 2008 (fig. 42B) for groundwater samples. Based on the inverse modeling, the flow to the deep system has dissolved calcite, dolomite, and CO_2 and the mass balance indicates that a majority of the carbon is from the addition of CO_2 (i.e., MOWE-East is 11.95 millimoles of carbon from CO_2 and 3.76 millimoles of carbon from calcite and dolomite). For the shallow Verde Formation waters (i.e., MOWE-Residence) the carbon addition is slightly more from carbonate dissolution and is 1.77 millimoles of carbon from additional CO_2 (probably from organic matter decay in the Verde Formation) and 2.57 millimoles of carbon from calcite and dolomite dissolution (appendix 3).

For the inverse modeling in PHREEQC, the best mass balance fits required the use of ^{13}C isotopes in all three sources (calcite, dolomite, CO_2) to be zero (appendix 3), as more depleted values did not result in any inverse models (mass balance could not be completed). The PHREEQC files allow for error to be included in the ^{13}C values. For the input sources (calcite, dolomite, CO_2), an error of ±2 per mil was used and for the final waters, a measurement error of ±1 per mil was used (except the MOWE-Residence run, which required an error of ±2 per mil). Previous measurements in the area have determined ^{13}C values in local carbonates to average -1.85 per mil and ranged from a maximum of +2.44 per mil and a minimum of -3.84 per mil (Wirt and DeWitt, 2005). A measured ^{13}C value for the added carbon dioxide is not available. However, Clark and Fritz, 1997 and Newell and others, 2005, both give references to volcanic-related CO_2 having ^{13}C values near -6 per mil ±3 per mil. The dissolution of CO_2 results in a fractionation of ^{13}C (see table 5.7 in Clark and Fritz, 1997) based on the carbonate species in solution. While the groundwater solution at depth is unknown, a calculation (appendix 3) using the carbonate species in sample MOWE-West-118 and an assumed CO_2 value of -6 per mil gives a groundwater solution with ^{13}C as -1.47 per mil in the dissolved organic carbon (the measured value was -2.0 per mil). Overall, the use of ^{13}C as 0.0 per mil ±2 per mil seems to be within a reasonable range.

The final PHREEQC inverse models were used directly in NETPATH (Plummer and others, 1994) using NetpathXL (http://wwwbrr.cr.usgs.gov/projects/GWC_coupled/netpath) to calculate a groundwater age via the output files that are created by the latest version of PREEQC-interative (PhreeqcI, http://wwwbrr.cr.usgs.gov/projects/GWC_coupled/phreeqc). NETPATH has calculations built into the software that calculate adjusted age dates based on the addition of "dead" carbon (no ^{14}C).

The simulations provided in appendix 3 all assume that the added carbon sources (calcite, dolomite, and carbon dioxide) do not have any ^{14}C due to the million-year plus age of the carbon. Based on using the Lodge sample as the recharge water, the adjusted age of the deep groundwaters range from 5,400 years to 13,300 years old compared to unadjusted ages of 18,300 to 22,500 (appendix 3). For the MOWE-Residence sample, the adjusted age is 18,900 years old compared to an unadjusted age of 24,400 years old (appendix 3). The MOWE-Residence sample has a much smaller adjustment in age because of the much smaller amount on "dead" carbon entering the system from deep source CO_2. One source of uncertainty is the ^{14}C value in the initial recharge waters and a variety of models are built into NETPATH for this purpose (Plummer and others, 1994). With the Lodge sample, using a ^{14}C value in the initial recharge waters as 100 pMC increases the final ages by approximately 3,000 for all samples.

Conceptual Model Summary

A conceptual model of groundwater flow along the A-A' cross section is summarized in figure 50. Figure 50 uses conceptual flow lines based on general knowledge of the hydrogeology and highlight water-rock interaction using strontium concentrations, strontium isotope ratios, and arsenic concentrations. The main geologic features to consider are the permeable basalts near the surface at the higher elevations, the permeable Redwall Limestone (Mr) at depth (elevation, and the low permeability basalt dike underneath Montezuma Well (MW in fig. 50).

Groundwater Modeling

Numerical Simulations

Numerical profile models (figs. 51, 52, and 53) of cross section A-A' (fig. 3) were constructed to more quantitatively test the conceptual model of groundwater flow near Montezuma Well presented in figure 50. MODFLOW-2000 (Harbaugh and others, 2000) was used to simulate steady-state groundwater flow in the cross section using different hydrogeologic conceptual models to evaluate the effect different subsurface geologic structures could have on flow to Montezuma well. Hydrogeologic conceptual models evaluated were 1) no subsurface geologic structure, 2) a vertical low-permeability geologic structure (basalt dike), 3) a vertical low-permeability subsurface geologic structure (basalt dike) with a drain to simulate Montezuma Well, and 4) a vertical high-permeability subsurface geologic structure. Because few water-level data were available for hydrogeologic layers simulated by the model, the model was not calibrated and was used only to evaluate general head distributions and groundwater flow patterns near Montezuma Well. Results of each of these hydrogeologic conceptual models are presented in this report and detailed conclusions will be provided in the subsequent journal article. All original MODFLOW files can be found in Appendix 4.

Model Design

The groundwater system near Montezuma Well is represented using a profile model (figs. 51, 52, and 53) about 15.9 mi long, extending from about 3.3 mi downgradient of Montezuma Well to about 12.6 mi upgradient of the well to Apache Maid Mountain (high point on A' side). The model simulates groundwater flow in a strip 100 feet (ft) wide and includes hydrogeologic layers and structures between ground surface and Precambrian basement rock at a depth ranging from about 1500 to 3400 ft below ground surface. The model grid has 95 rows and 167 columns with a cell size of 500 ft (horizontal) x 200 ft (vertical). Model vertical dimension is 4 times greater than actual to better display vertical flow in the groundwater system. Because all hydrogeologic layers are exaggerated by the same factor, relative flow patterns are similar to those for a model with no vertical exaggeration.

The downgradient portion of the model is simulated as a constant-head boundary to allow flow out of the simulated groundwater system. The base and upgradient end of the model are simulated as no-flow boundaries to represent Precambrian basement rock and low-permeability igneous stock below Apache Maid Mountain (high point on A' side in fig. 50). Cells above the potentiometric surface at the top of the model are inactive and are treated as no-flow cells. One cell in the top hydrogeologic layer at the upgradient end of the model has constant head equal to the estimated water level near Apache Maid Mountain in order to establish hydraulic-head gradients across the model representative of the groundwater system in the study area. The model simulates flow under confined conditions.

Hydraulic conductivity of each hydrogeologic layer was estimated using typical values presented in the literature (Freeze and Cherry, 1979) for each rock type. Hydrogeologic layers estimated to have moderate hydraulic conductivity (fig. 50) are assigned a value of 0.05 feet/day (ft/d). Hydrogeologic layers estimated to have high hydraulic conductivity are assigned a value of 0.5 ft/d. Hydrogeologic layers estimated to have very high hydraulic conductivity are assigned a value of 10 ft/d. Vertical geologic structures evaluated near Montezuma Well are simulated using the Horizontal-Flow Barrier package (Hsieh and Freckleton, 1993) for MODFLOW. Recharge is not simulated by the model.

Simulation Results

Simulation 1

Simulation 1 represents general hydraulic head and flow conditions in the groundwater system without the presence of a geologic structure (no basalt dike) near Montezuma Well. The simulated hydraulic head and groundwater flow directions for simulation 1 are shown in figure 51.

Simulation 2

Simulation 2 (fig. 52) shows the effect of a vertical low-permeability subsurface geologic structure (basalt dike) immediately downgradient from Montezuma Well. The geologic structure is simulated as a 75-ft-thick vertical barrier extending from the model base upward about 800 ft to the very-high hydraulic conductivity layer that intersects the upper model layers. The structure is simulated as having hydraulic conductivity equal to 0.00028 ft/d.

Simulation 2 was rerun using a low-permeability structure with a vertical extent ranging from about 400 - 1400 ft, where the 1400-ft structure extends to the simulated land surface (GRABHB folder in Appenix 4). The shorter structure causes less groundwater to flow upward toward Montezuma Well. The structure that extends to land surface causes more upward flow toward the well and creates unrealistic head conditions as ground water mounds upgradient of the structure and greatly declines downgradient of the structure. Simulation 2 also was rerun using a different location for the low-permeability structure. The structure was moved about 0.8 mi downgradient of Montezuma Well to represent the right side of a fault-bounded graben at that location (LOWKHB2 folder in Appendix 4). Simulated hydraulic head and flow conditions resulting from the different structure configuration and location are similar to those from the original location except that upward groundwater flow from the deeper layers occurs downgradient of Montezuma Well, resulting in little to no flow to the Montezuma Well from the deeper layers. Files from these reruns are included in Appendix 4, but not included in any figures.

Simulation 3

Simulation 3 (fig. 53) represents the conditions of simulation 2 with the addition of drain cells in the buried basalt channel. These drain cells are intended to simulate the conditions created by Montezuma Well (head is set to the pond level at 3,573 feet), which is presumably fed by a fracture system at depth. Because of the excess carbon dioxide, this fracture system may be self-sealing near the surface as carbon dioxide degasses and calcite precipitates. Therefore, drain cells in the simulation are only located in the subsurface basalt channel and are not extended to the surface.

Simulation 4

Simulation 4 represents hydraulic head and flow conditions resulting from the presence of a vertical high-permeability (hydraulic conductivity = 100 ft/d) subsurface geologic structure immediately downgradient from Montezuma Well. The presence of a high-permeability structure near Montezuma Well had no substantial effect on hydraulic head and flow in the groundwater system, and results are nearly identical to those presented in fig. 51 for simulation 1. Therefore, a separate figure is not presented. Simulation 4 was rerun using a high-permeability structure with different vertical extents (HIGHKHB2 folder in Appendix 4), but none of the simulations resulted in any significant changes in hydraulic head or flow in the groundwater system.

Summary

This report releases data collected in 2006 and 2008 from water and rock samples in and around Montezuma Well. Newly developed geologic cross sections and groundwater flow modeling to assist in identifying the source of groundwater to Montezuma Well are also presented. All methodologies and data results are provided herein with interpretations to be provided in separate journal articles.

References Cited

Appelo, C.A.J., and Postma, D., 2005, Geochemistry, groundwater and pollution (2d ed.): Leiden, Balkema, 649 p.

Bayer, R., Schlosser, P., Bonisch, G., Rupp, H., Zaucker, F., and Zimmek, G., 1989, Performance and blank components of a mass spectrometric system routine measurement of helium isotopes and tritium by ^{3}He ingrowth method, *in* Sitzungsberichte der Heidelberger Akademie der Wissenschaften—Mathematisch-naturwissenschaftliche Klasse [Proceedings]: Heidelberg, Springer Verlang, p. 241–279.

Briggs, P.H., 2002a, The determination of twenty-seven elements in aqueous samples by inductively coupled plasma–atomic emission spectrometry, chap. F *of* Taggart, J.E., ed., Analytical methods for chemical analysis of geologic and other materials, U.S. Geological Survey: U.S. Geological Survey Open-File Report 02–223–F, 11 p. (also available at *http://pubs.usgs.gov/of/2002/ofr-02-0223/F0203ICPAES_M.pdf*).

Briggs, P.H., 2002b, The determination of forty elements in geological and botanical samples by inductively coupled plasma–atomic emission spectrometry, chap. G *of* Taggart, J.E., ed., Analytical methods for chemical analysis of geologic and other materials, U.S. Geological Survey: U.S. Geological Survey Open-File Report 02–223–G, 18 p. (also available at *http://pubs.usgs.gov/of/2002/ofr-02-0223/G01fortyelementICP-AESsolid_M.pdf*).

Briggs, P.H., and Meier, A.L., 2002, The determination of forty-two elements in geological materials by inductively coupled plasma–mass spectrometry, chap. I *of* Taggart, J.E., ed., Analytical methods for chemical analysis of geologic and other materials, U.S. Geological Survey: U.S. Geological Survey

Open-File Report 02–223–I, 14 p. (also available at *http://pubs.usgs.gov/of/2002/ofr-02-0223/I20NAWQAPlus_M.pdf*).

Clark, I.D., and Fritz, Peter, 1997, Environmental isotopes in hydrogeology: New York, Lewis Publishers, 328 p.

Corns, W.T., Stockwell, P.B., Ebdon, Les, and Hill, S.J., 1993, Development of an atomic fluorescence spectrometer for the hydride-forming elements: Journal of Analytical Atomic Spectrometry, v. 8, p. 71–77.

Demange, D., Grivet, M., Pialot, H., and Chambaudet, A., 2002, Indirect tritium determination by an original ^{3}He ingrowth method using a standard helium leak detector mass spectrometer: Analytical Chemistry, v. 74, p. 3183–3189.

Donchin, J.H., 1983, Stratigraphy and sedimentary environments of the Miocene-Pliocene Verde Formation in southeastern Verde Valley, Yavapai County, Arizona: Flagstaff, Ariz., Northern Arizona University, M.S. thesis, 182 p.

Epstein, S., and Mayeda, T., 1953, Variations of O_{18} contents of waters from natural sources: Geochimica et Cosmochimica Acta, v. 4, p. 213–224.

Freeze, R.A., and Cherry, J.A., 1979, Groundwater: Englewood Cliffs, N.J., Prentice-Hall, Inc., 604 p.

Harbaugh, A.W., Banta, E.R., Hill M.C., and McDonald, M.G., 2000, MODFLOW-2000, the U.S. Geological Survey modular ground-water model—User guide to modularization concepts and the ground-water flow process: U.S. Geological Survey Open-File Report 00–92, 121 p.

Hsieh, P.A., and Freckleton, J.R., 1993, Documentation of a computer program to simulate horizontal-flow barriers using the U.S. Geological Survey modular three-dimensional finite-difference ground-water flow model: U.S. Geological Survey Open-File Report 92–477, 32 p.

Kendall, Carol, and Coplen, T.B., 1985, Multi-sample conversion of water to hydrogen by zinc for stable isotope determination: Analytical Chemistry, v. 57, no. 7, p. 1437–1440.

Koneiczki, A.D., and Leake, S.A., 1997, Hydrogeology and water chemistry of Montezuma Well in Montezuma Castle National Monument and surrounding area, Arizona: U.S. Geological Survey Water Resources Investigations Report 97–4156, 49 p.

Lamothe, P.J., Meier, A.L., and Wilson, S.A., 2002, The determination of forty-four elements in aqueous samples by inductively coupled plasma–mass spectrometry, chap. H *of* Taggart, J.E., ed., Analytical methods for chemical analysis of geologic and other materials, U.S. Geological Survey: U.S. Geological Survey Open-File Report 02–223–H, 11 p. (also available at *http://pubs.usgs.gov/of/2002/ofr-02-0223/H21&23OFR99-151_M.pdf*).

Lange, A., 1957, Studies on the origin of Montezuma Well and Cave, Arizona: Cave Studies—Publication of the Western Speleological Institute, v. 1, no. 9, p. 31-45. [Manuscript in the files of the University of Arizona Special Collections.]

McKee, E.D., Hastings, Homer, and Colton, H.S., 1947, Montezuma's Well, result of preliminary soundings, July 18, 1947 [unpublished manuscript]: Flagstaff, Ariz., Museum of Northern Arizona archives.

Moreno, E., Camara, C., Corns, W.T., Bryce, D.W., and Stockwell, P.B., 2000, Arsenic speciation in beverages by direct injection-ion chromatography—Hydride generation atomic fluorescence spectrometry: Journal of Automated Methods & Management in Chemistry, v. 22, p. 33–39.

Newell, D.L., Crossey, L.J., Karlstrom, K.E., and Fischer, T.P., 2005, Continental-scale links between the mantle and groundwater systems of the western United States—Evidence from travertine springs and regional He isotope data: GSA Today, v. 15, no. 12, p. 4–10.

Parkhurst, D.L., and Appelo, C.A.J., 1999, User's guide to PHREEQC (version 2)—A computer program for speciation, batch-reaction, one-dimensional transport, and inverse geochemical calculations: U.S. Geological Survey Water-Resource Investigations Report 99–4259, 312 p.

Plummer, L.N., Prestemon, E.C., Parkhurst, D.L., 1994, An interactive code (NETPATH) for modeling NET geochemical reactions along a flowpath, version 2.0: U.S. Geological Survey Water-Resource Investigations Report 94–4169, 130 p.

Ranney, W.D.R., 2001, Sedona through time geology of the red rocks: Flagstaff, Ariz., Zia Interpretive Services, 104 p.

Taylor, C.D., and Theodorakos, P.M., 2002, Rock sample preparation, chap. A1 *of* Taggart, J.E., ed., Analytical methods for chemical analysis of geologic and other materials, U.S. Geological Survey: U.S. Geological Survey Open-File Report 02–223–A1, 5 p. (also available at *http://pubs.usgs.gov/of/2002/ofr-02-0223/A1RxSampPrep_M.pdf*).

Theodorakos, P.M., d'Angelo, W.M., and Ficklin, W.H., 2002, Fluoride, chloride, nitrate, and sulfate in aqueous solution utilizing autosuppression chemically suppressed ion chromatography, chap. V *of* Taggart, J.E., ed., Analytical methods for chemical analysis of geologic and other materials, U.S. Geological Survey: U.S. Geological Survey Open-File Report 02–223–V, 7 p. (also available at *http://pubs.usgs.gov/of/2002/ofr-02-0223/OFR-02-0223.pdf*).

Twenter, F.R., and Metzger, D.G., 1963, Geology and ground water in Verde Valley—The Mogollon Rim region Arizona: U.S. Geological Survey Bulletin 1177, 132 p.

Weir, G.W., Ulrich, G.E., and Nealey, L.D., 1989, Geologic map of the Sedona 30' x 60' quadrangle, Yavapai and Coconino counties, Arizona: U.S. Geological Survey Miscellaneous Investigations Series Map I-1896m, scale 1:100,000.

Wirt, Laurie, and DeWitt, Ed, 2005, Geochemistry of major aquifers and springs, *in* Wirt, Laurie, DeWitt, Ed, and Langeheim, V.E., eds., Geologic framework of aquifer units and ground-water flowpaths in the Verde River Headwaters, north-central Arizona: U.S. Geological Survey Open-File Report 2004–1411, 44 p.

Figures

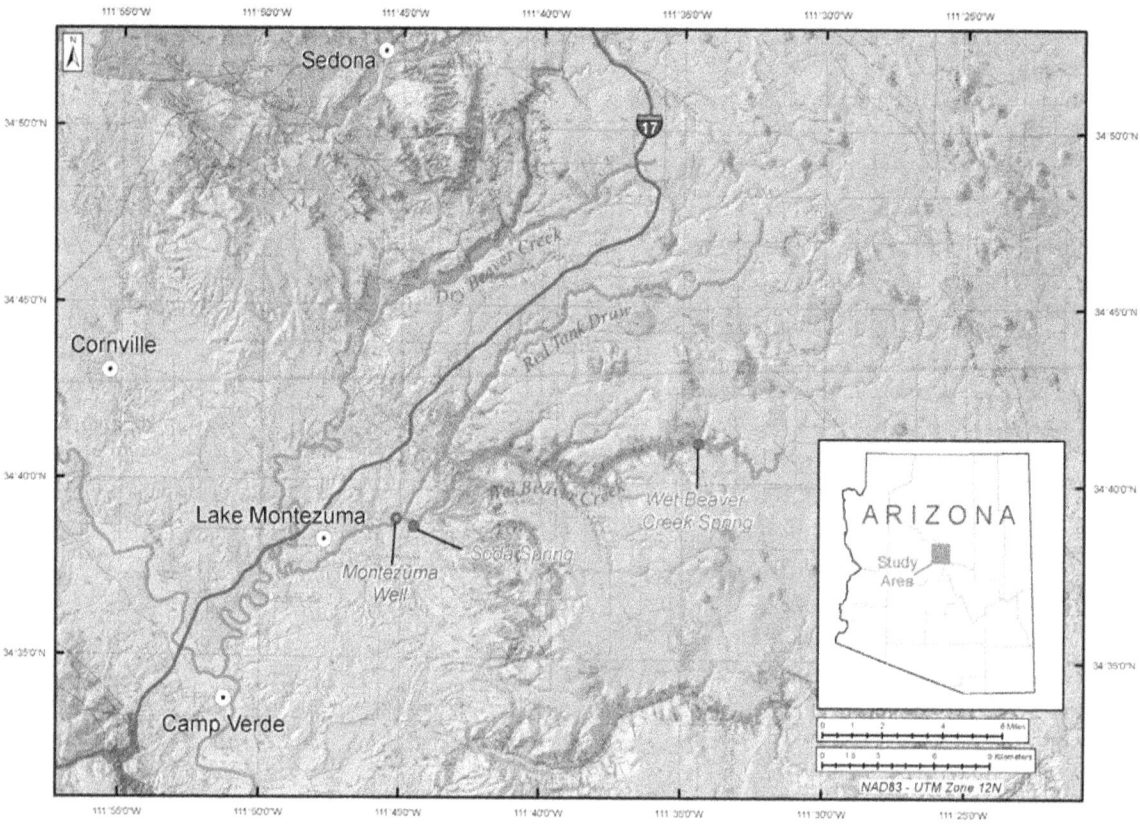

Figure 1.   Location and details of study area overlain on geologic map by Weir and others (1989) with hillshade elevations. [Yellow/black dots are towns, blue dots and circles are springs.]

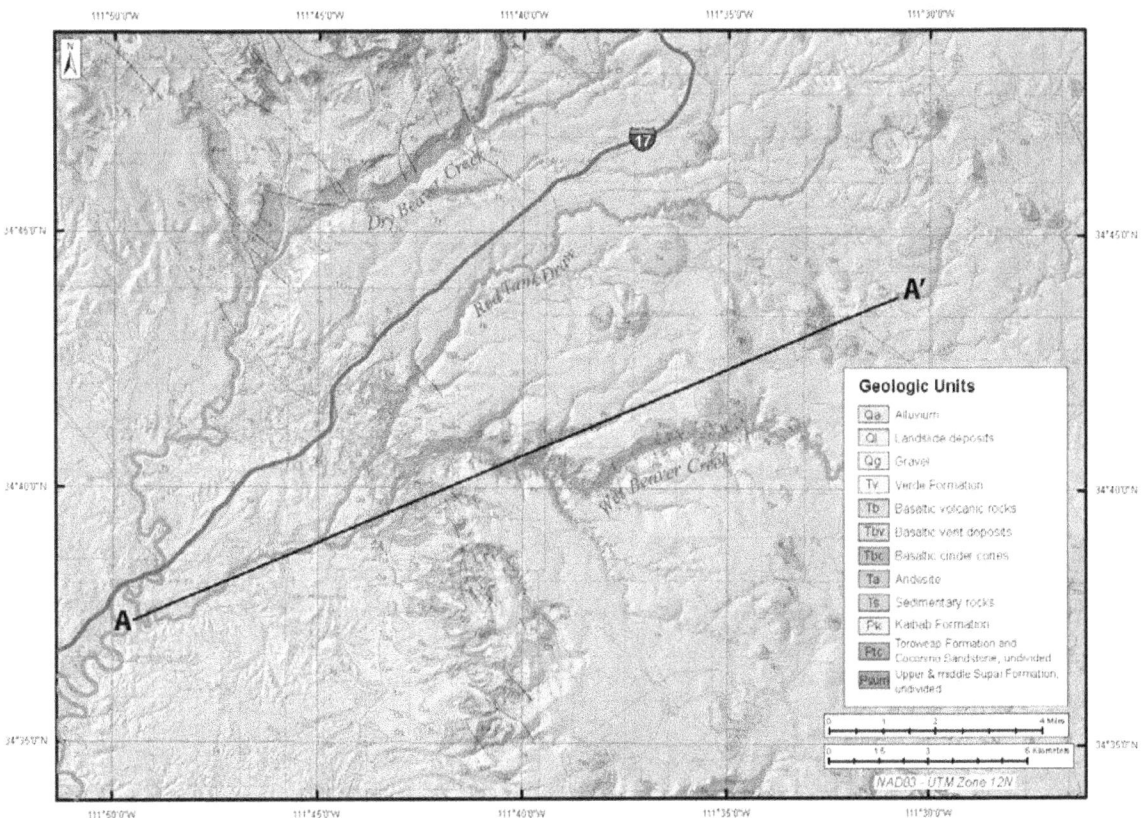

Figure 2.   Geologic map by Weir and others (1989) with cross-section location and hillshade elevations.

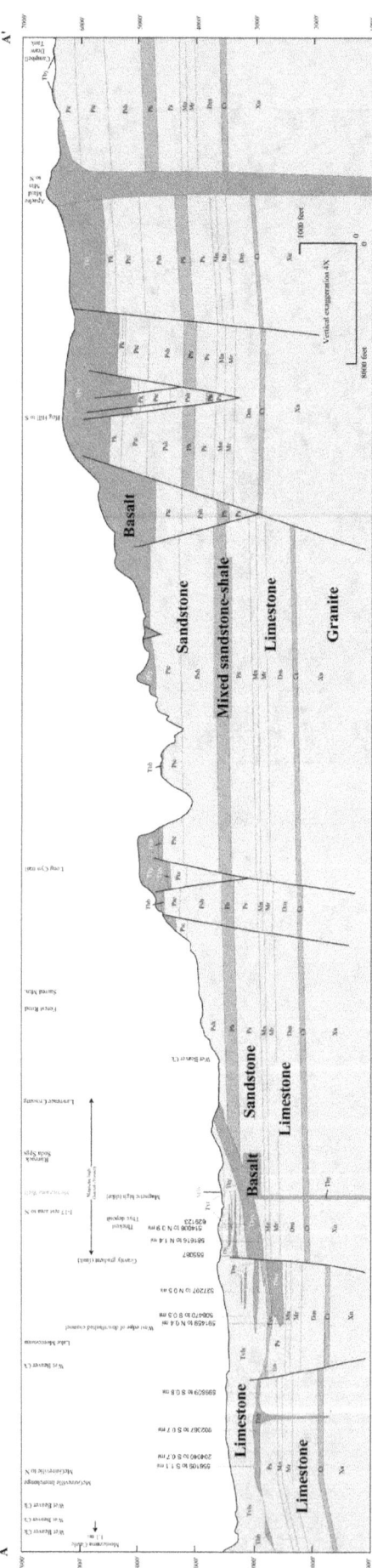

EXPLANATION

Tby	younger basalt (4-6 Ma)
Tvt	travertine in the Tertiary Verde Formation
Tvls	limestone in the Tertiary Verde Formation
Tvc	conglomerate in the Tertiary Verde Formation
Tbyc	younger basalt and conglomerate in the Tertiary Verde Formation
Thb	basalt in the Tertiary Hickey Formation
Pk	Permian Kaibab Formation
Ptc	Permian Toroweap and Coconino Sandstone
Psh	Permian Shenebly Hill Formation
Ph	Permian Hermit Shale
Ps	Permian and Pennsylvanian Supai Formation
Mn	Mississippian Naco Formation
Mr	Mississippian Redwall Limestone
Dm	Devonian Martin Formation
Ct	Cambrian Tapeats Sandstone
Xu	Early Proterozoic basement rocks, undifferentiated

556109, Arizona Department of Water Resources 55-series number of water wells used in cross section

MW, Montezuma Well

Figure 3. Geologic cross section along A-A' located in figure 2 with major rock types.

16

-400   -300   -200   -100   0   100   200   300   400   500   nano Teslas

least magnetic

most magnetic

+   Major magnetic inflection

+   Minor magnetic inflection

Gravity contours at 2-milligal interval

Major highway (white)

Secondary road (white)

Body of water

O   Spring

Aeromagnetic map enlarged from Langenheim and others (2005)

Figure 4.   Aeromagnetic map of Montezuma Well area, Verde Valley.

17

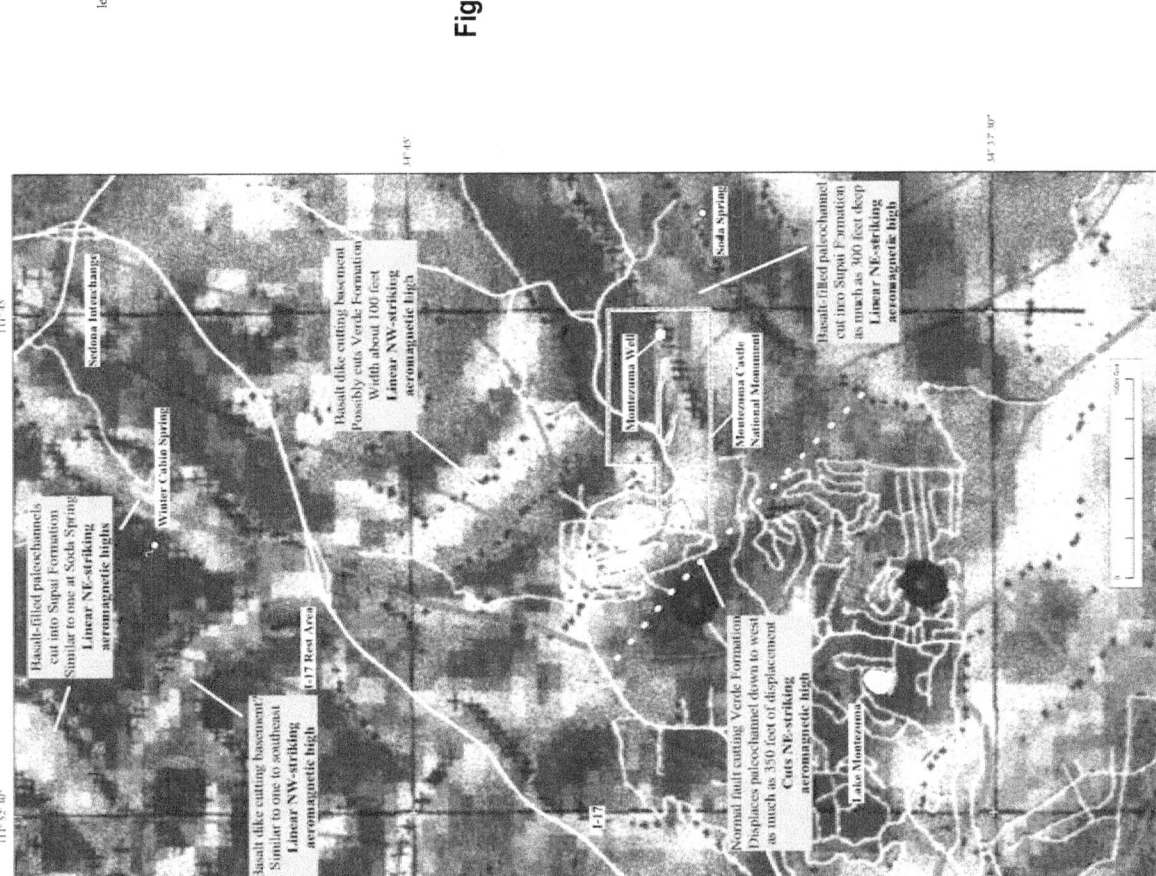

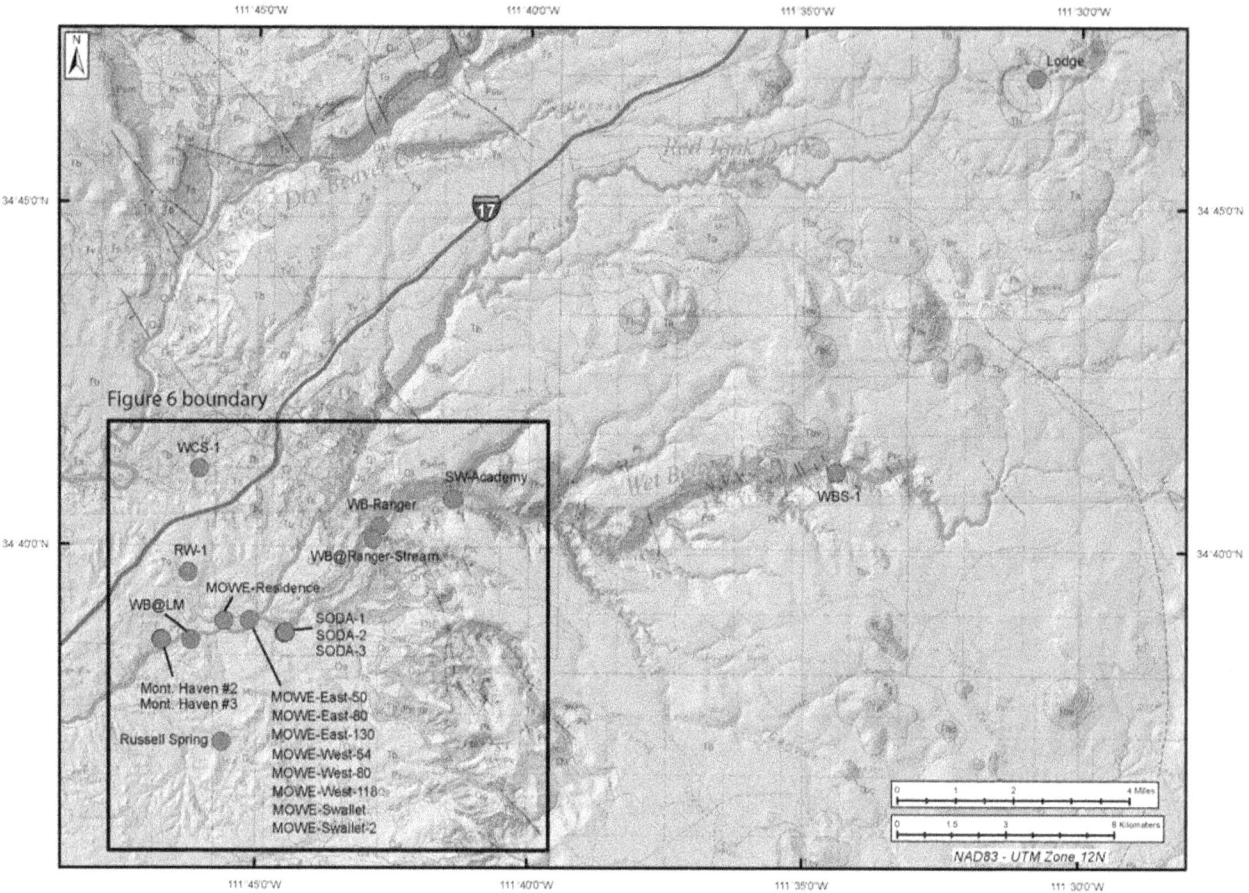

Figure 5. Location of water samples from 2006 with area of figure 6 outlined.

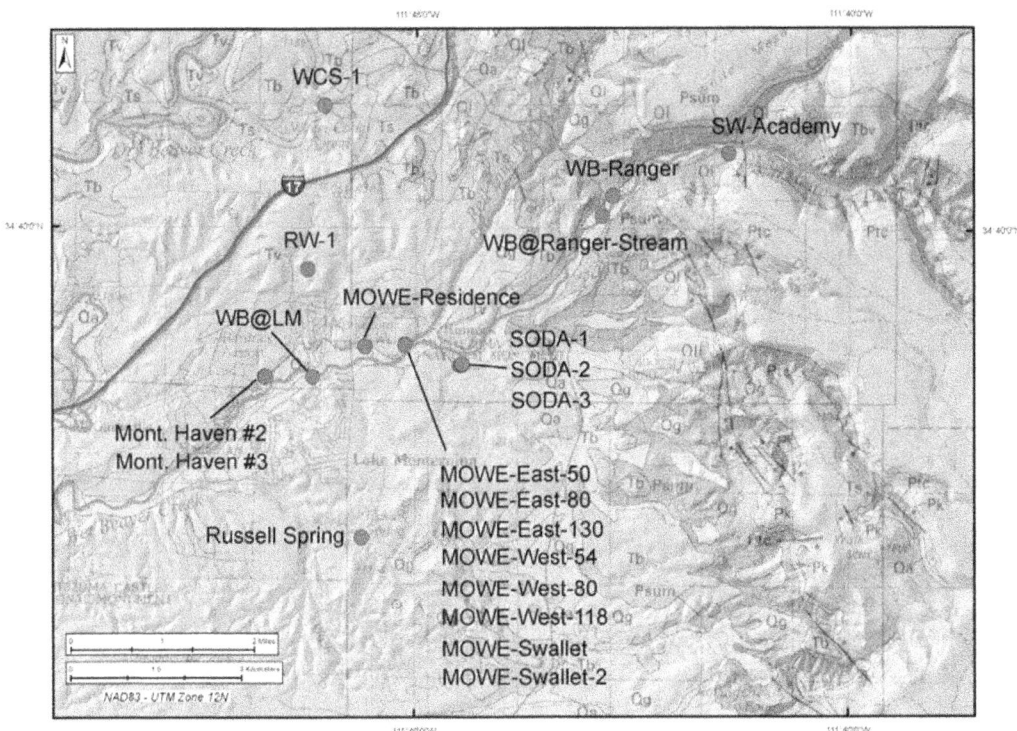

Figure 6. Location of water samples from 2006 in immediate Montezuma Well vicinity.

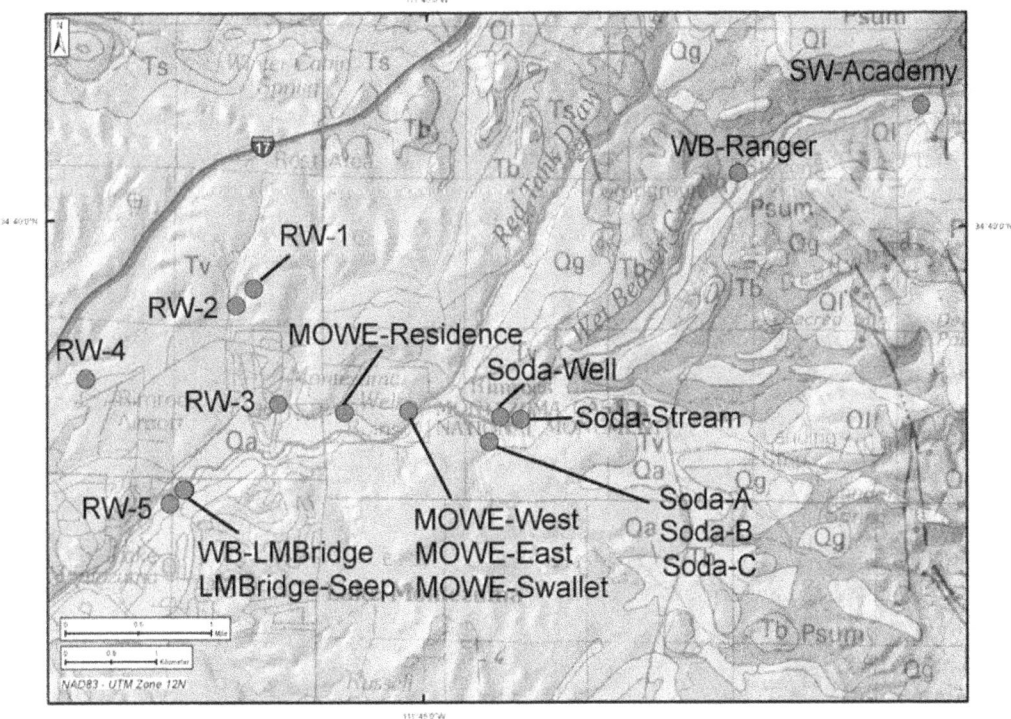

Figure 7. Location of water samples from 2008 in immediate Montezuma Well vicinity.

Peristaltic pump

Tubing and lines to surface

Well screen

YSI Hydrolab

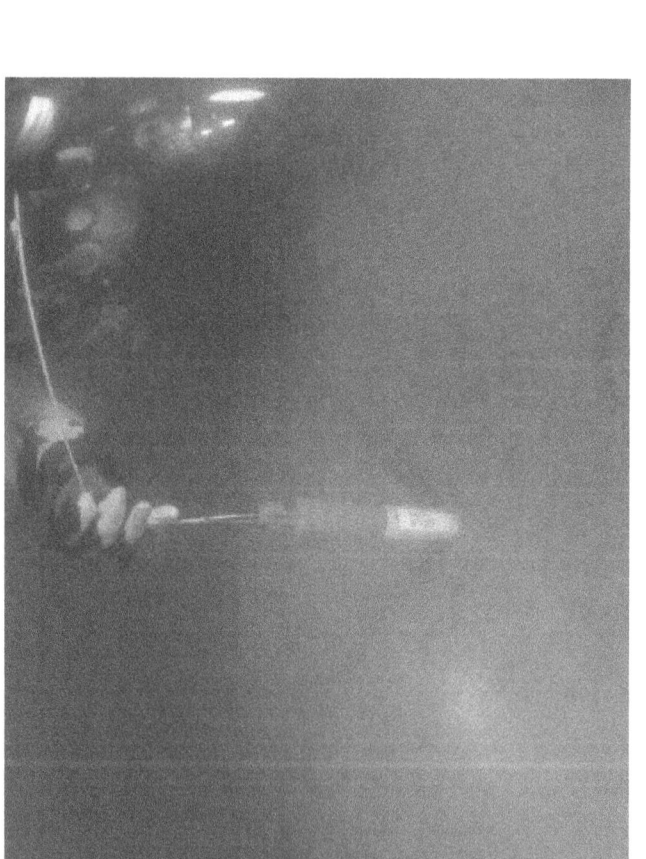

Figure 8. (Above) Photo of flowing sand "spring" at the "false bottom" of Montezuma Well with diver lowering a YSI Hydrolab. Photo courtesy of National Park Service Submerged Resources Center.

Figure 9. (Right) Photo of sampling apparatus with well screen attached to tubing that goes to a peristaltic pump (stays at surface in boat). YSI Hydrolab is also shown.

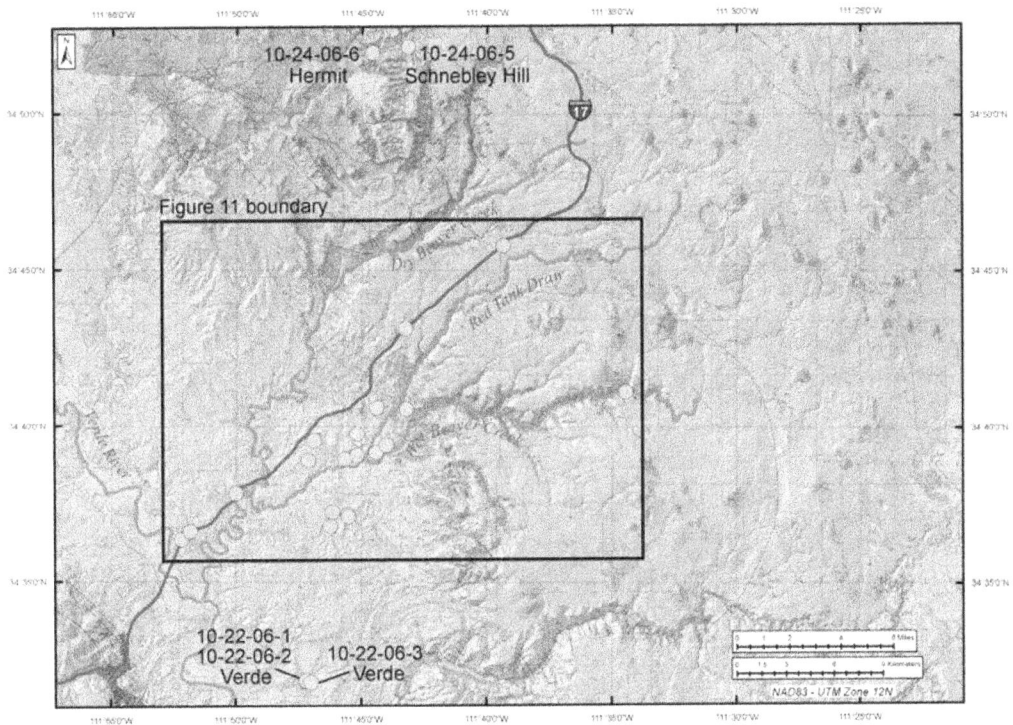

Figure 10. Location of rock samples with area of figure 11 outlined.

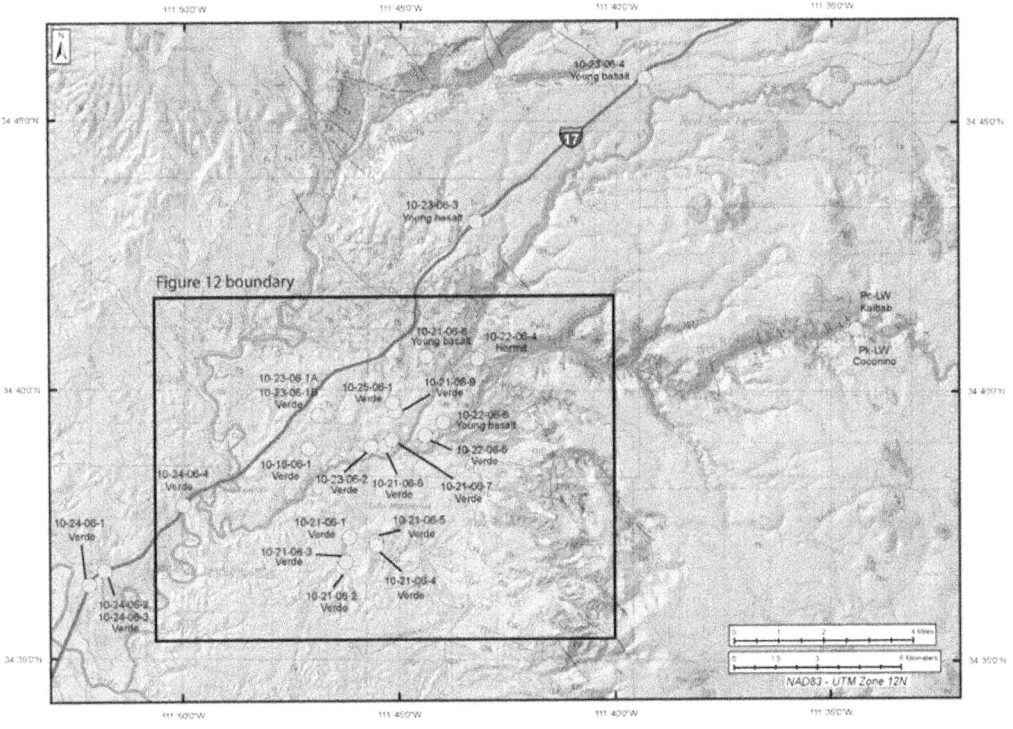

Figure 11. Location of rock samples with area of figure 12 outlined.

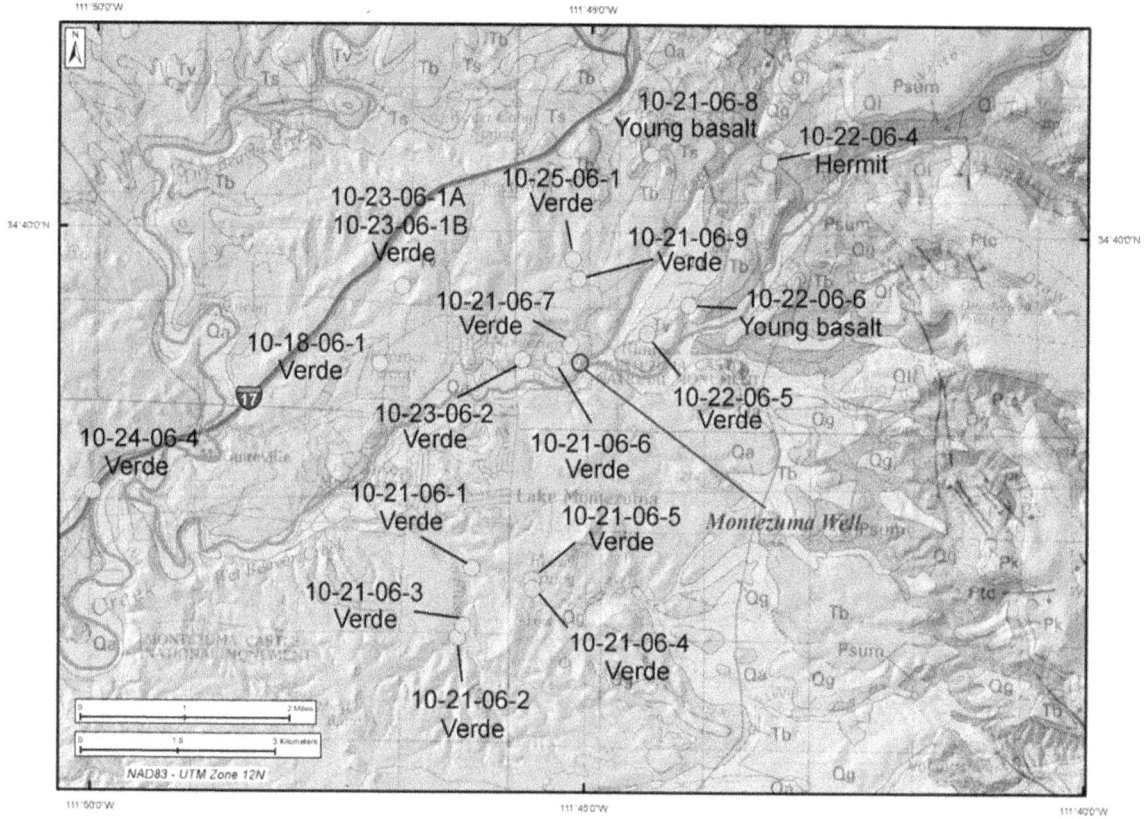

Figure 12. Location of rock samples in immediate Montezuma Well vicinity.

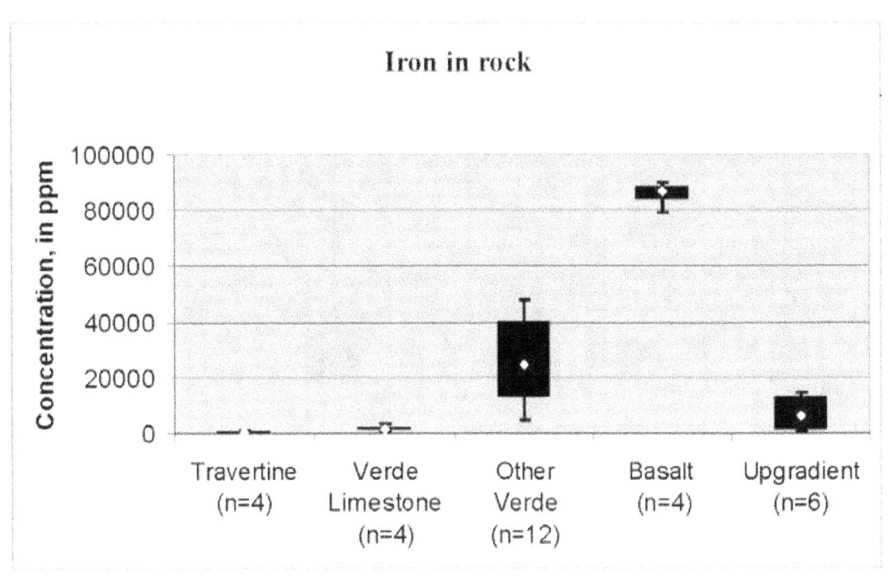

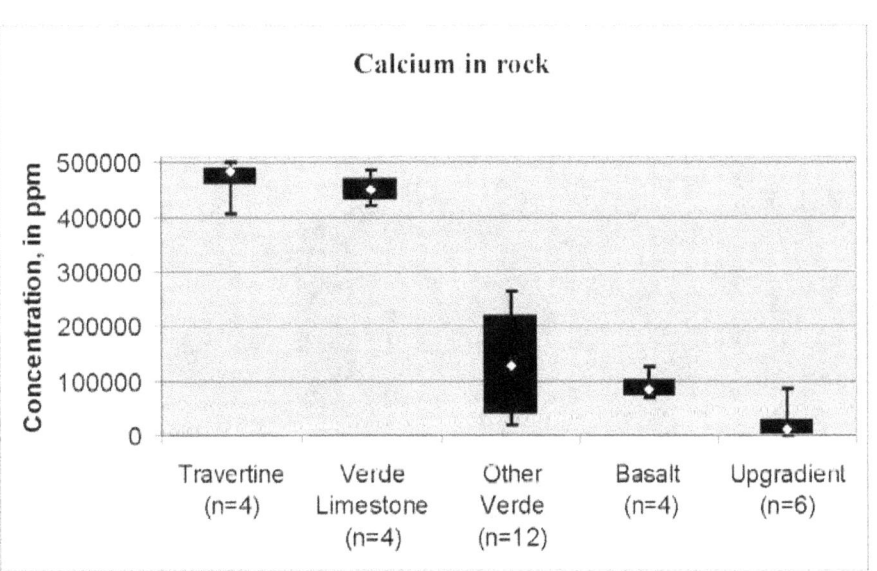

Figure 13. Concentrations of iron (Fe) and calcium (Ca) in rock samples.

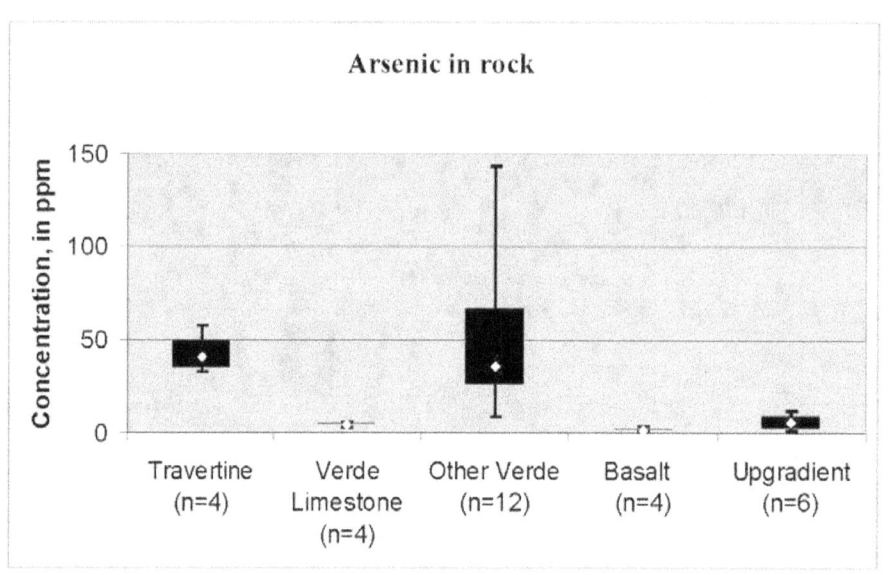

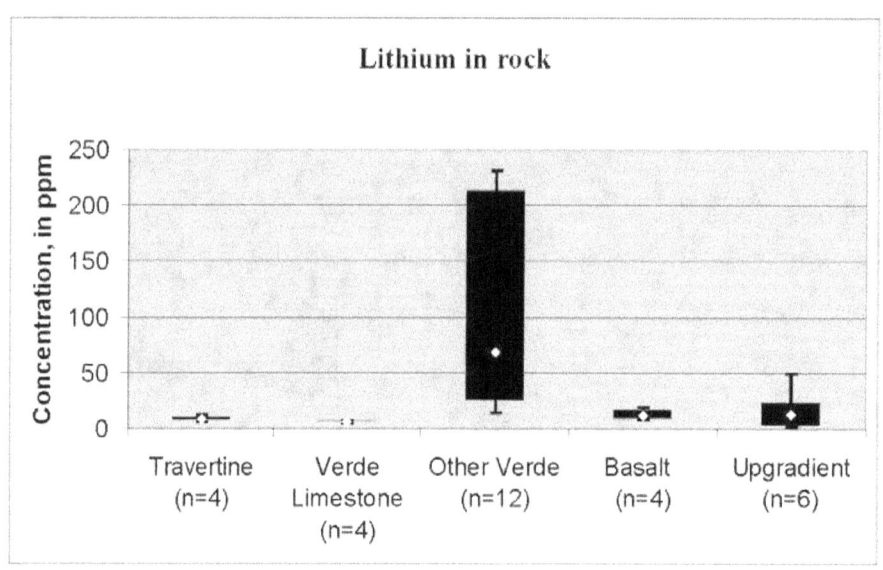

Figure 14. Concentrations of arsenic (As) and lithium (Li) in rock samples.

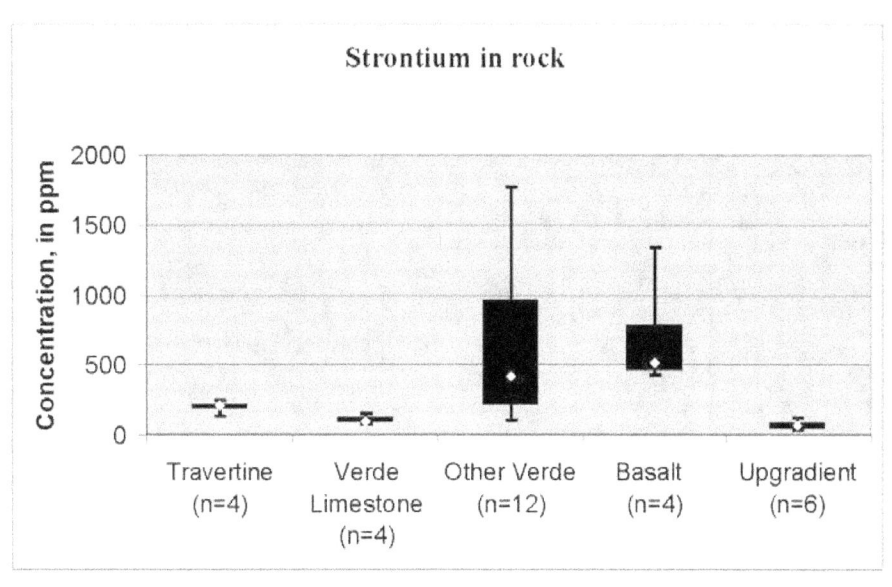

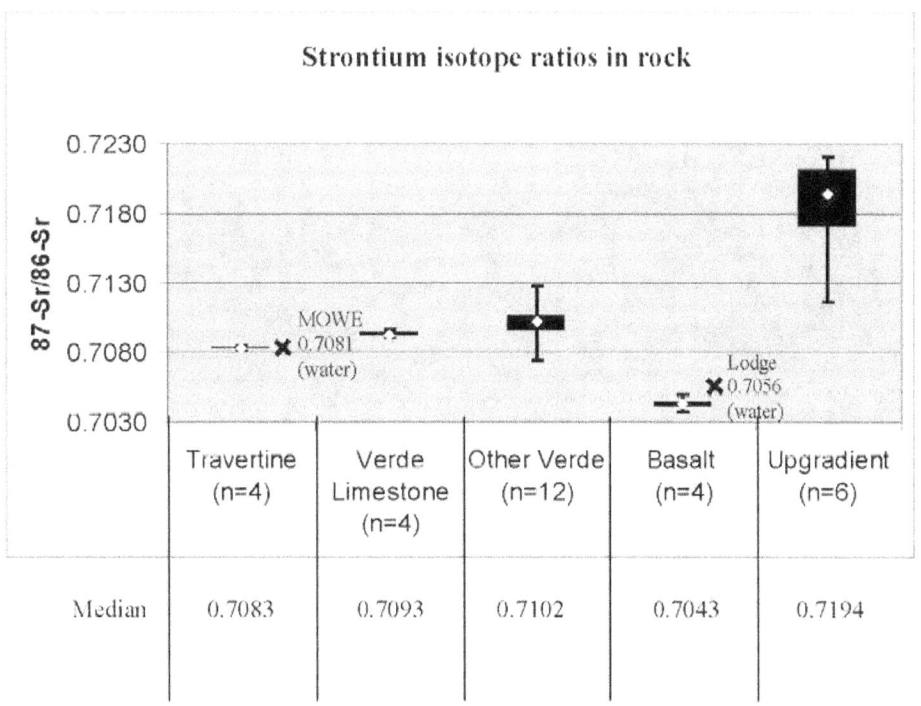

Figure 15. Concentrations of strontium (Sr) and strontium isotopes in rock samples.

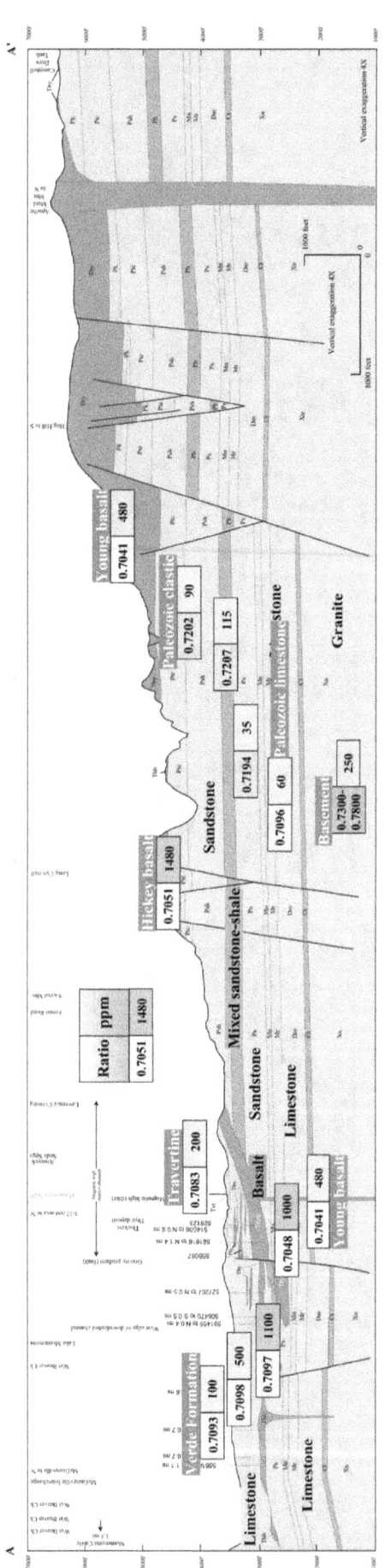

Figure 16. Strontium concentrations and isotopic ratios of major rock types along cross section A-A'.

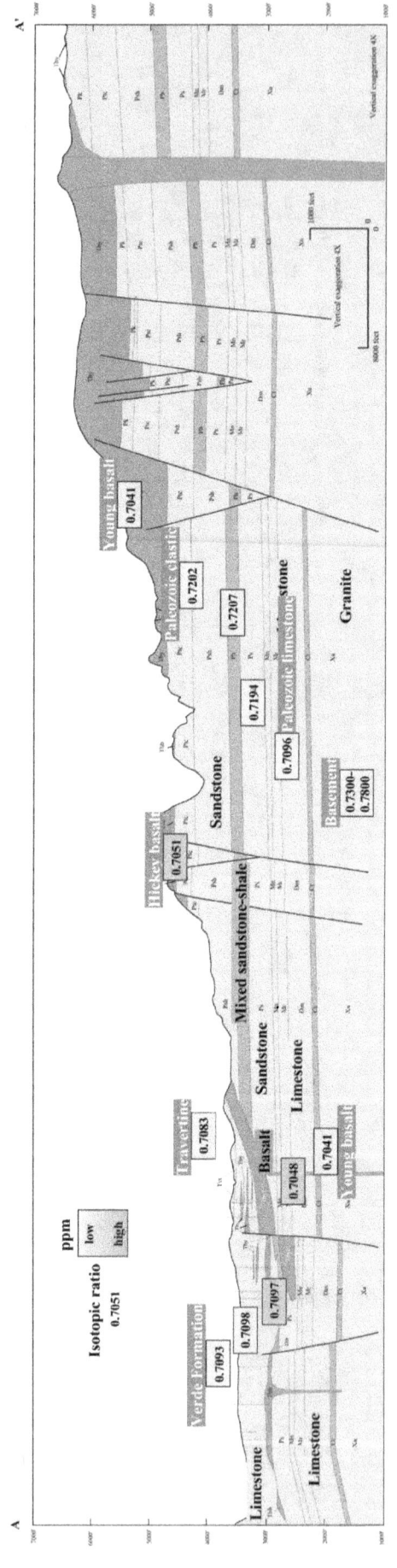

Figure 17. Strontium isotopes ratios of major rock types along cross section A-A'.

26

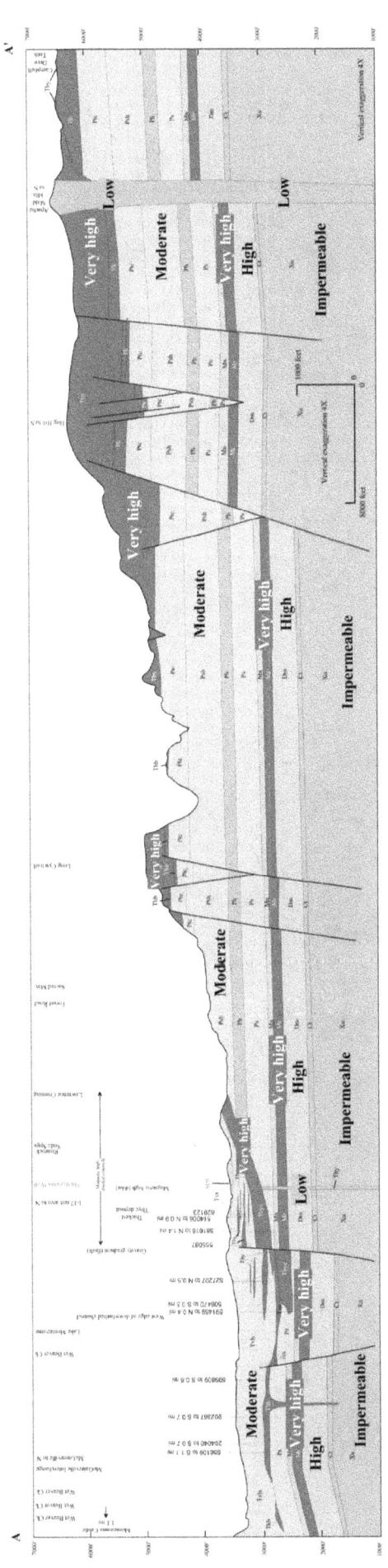

Figure 18. Permeabilities of rock units along cross section A-A'.

27

A

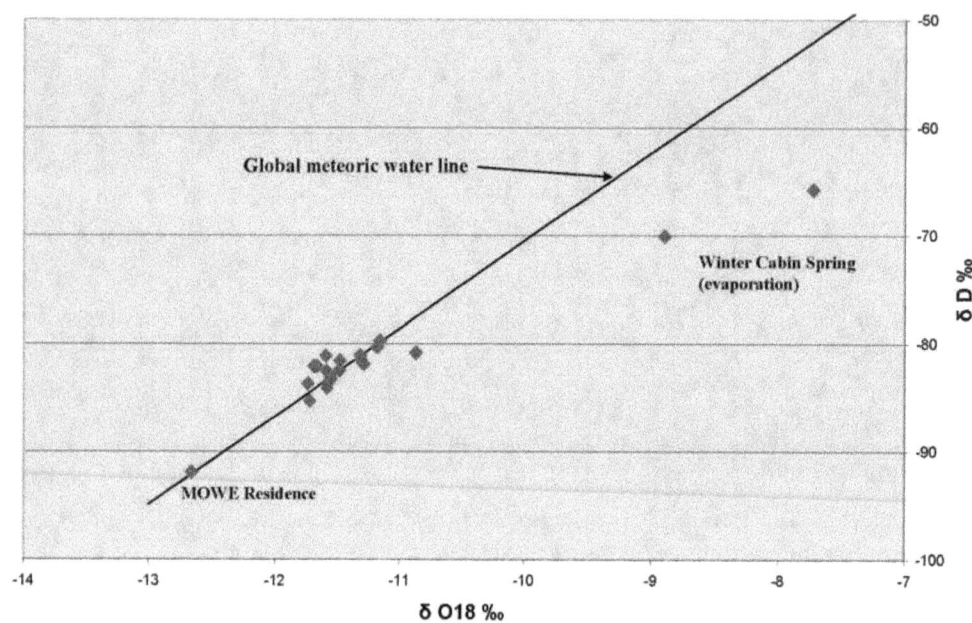

B

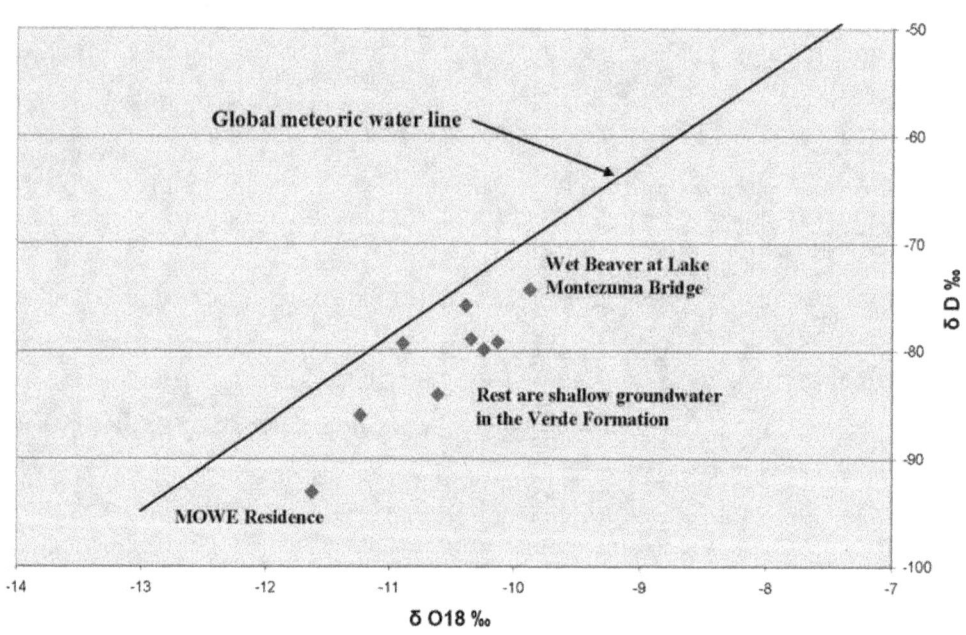

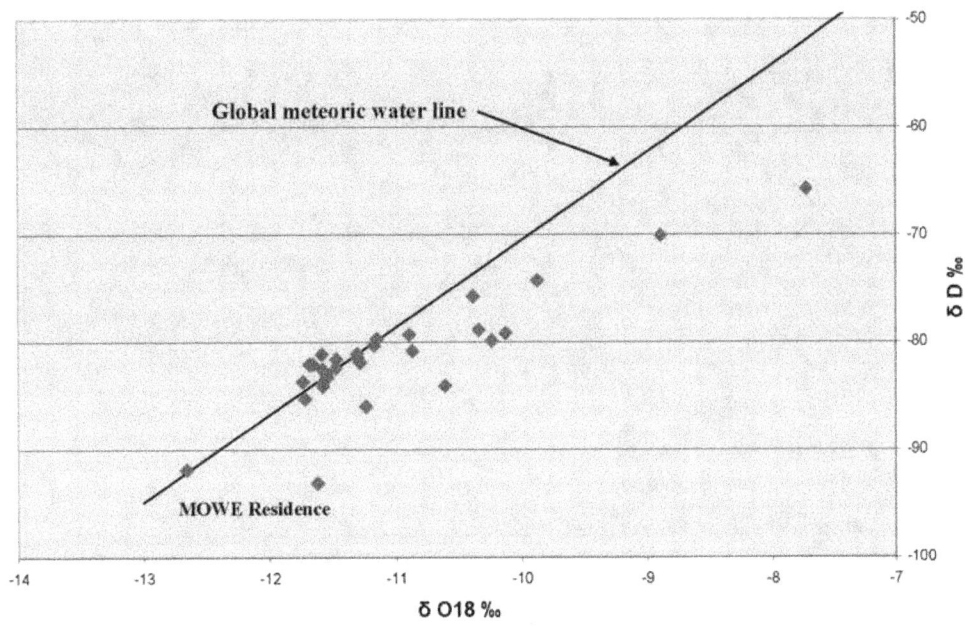

Figure 19. Oxygen and deuterium isotopes in water samples. *A*, 2006 samples. *B*, 2008 samples. *C*, 2006 and 2008 samples.

A

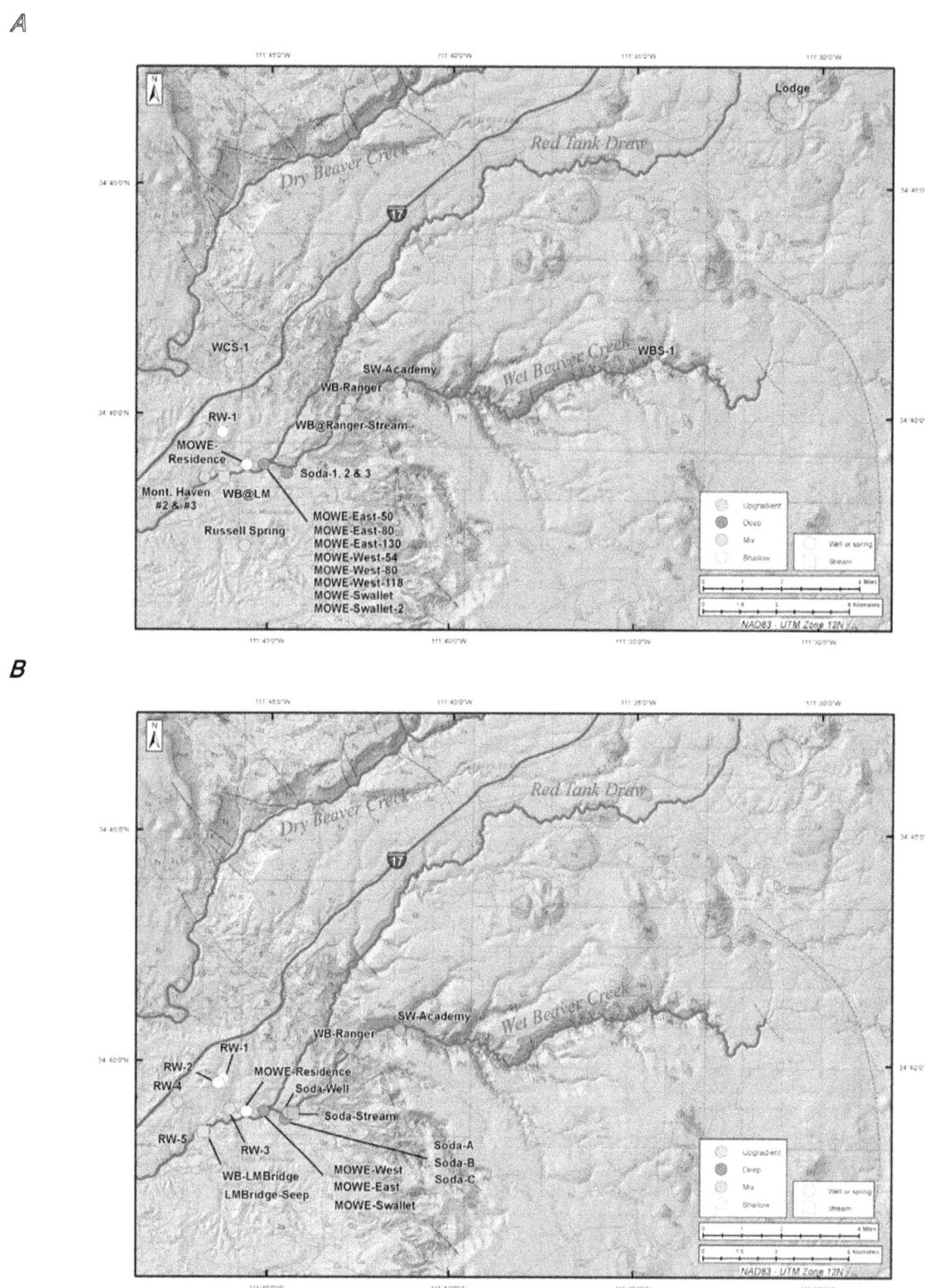

B

Figure 20. Sample categories and field numbers. *A*, 2006 data. *B*, 2008 data.

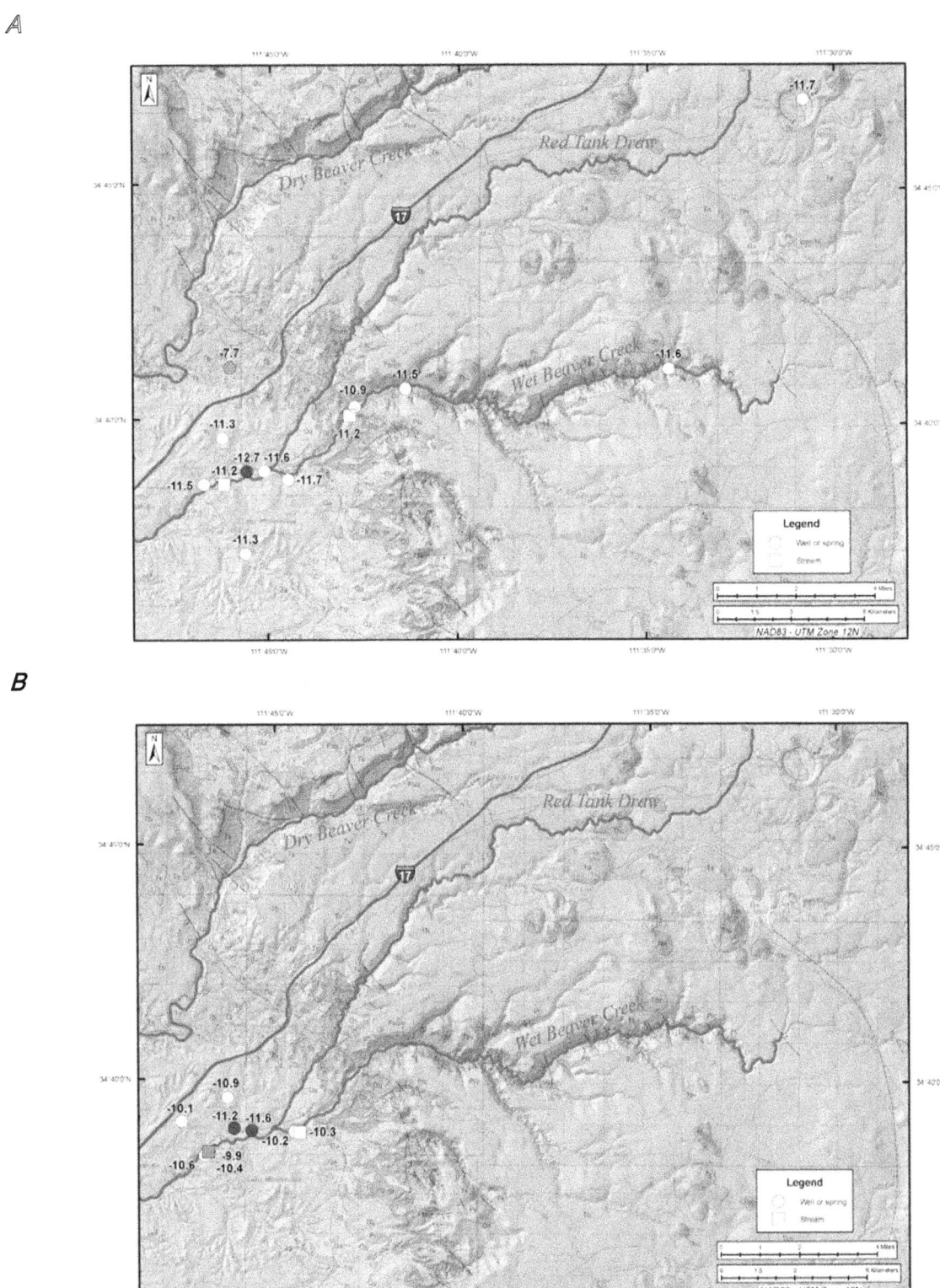

Figure 21. Oxygen isotope ($\delta^{18}O$) in per mil. *A*, 2006 data. *B*, 2008 data.

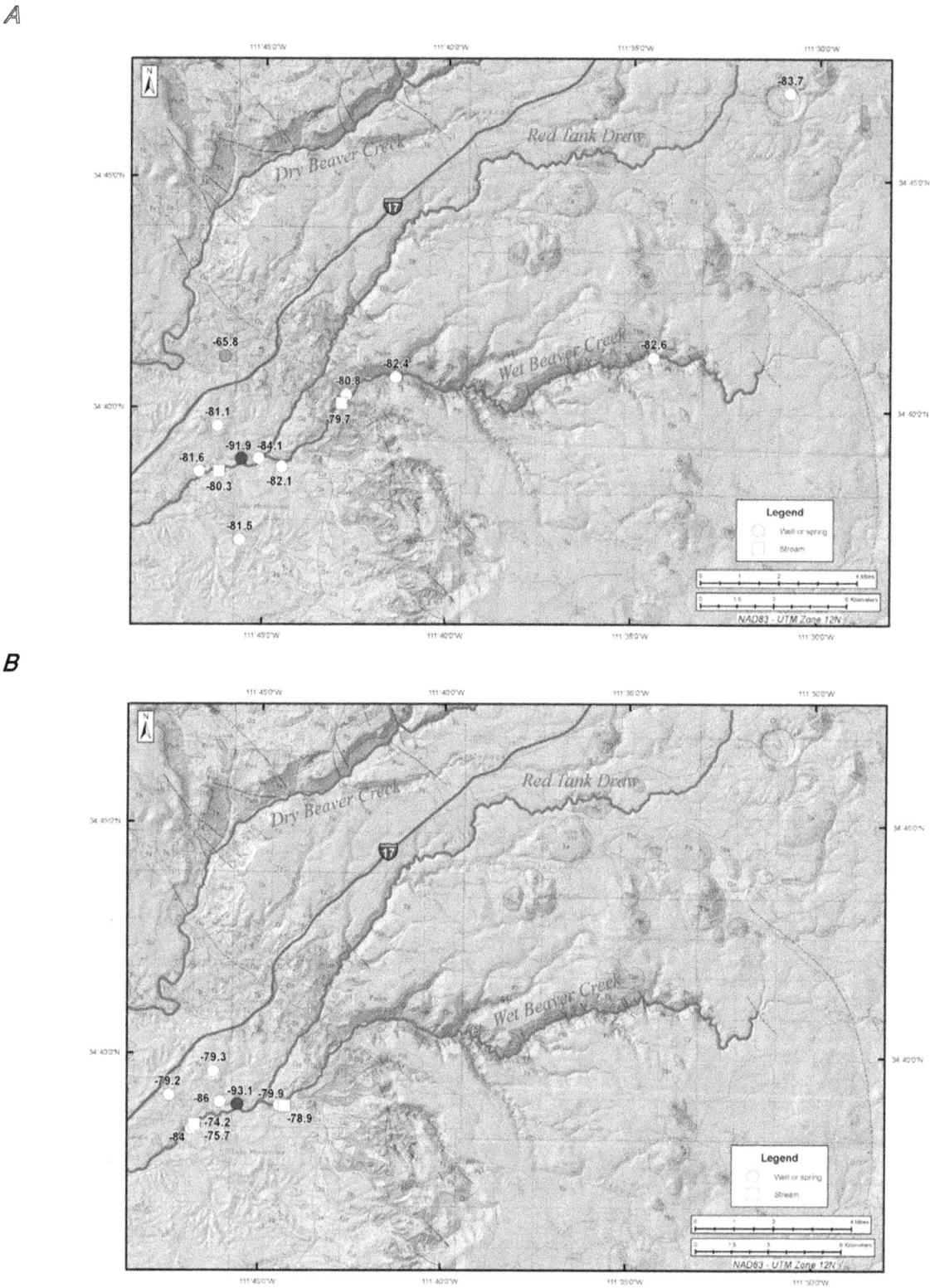

Figure 22. Deuterium isotope (δD) in per mil. *A*, 2006 data. *B*, 2008 data.

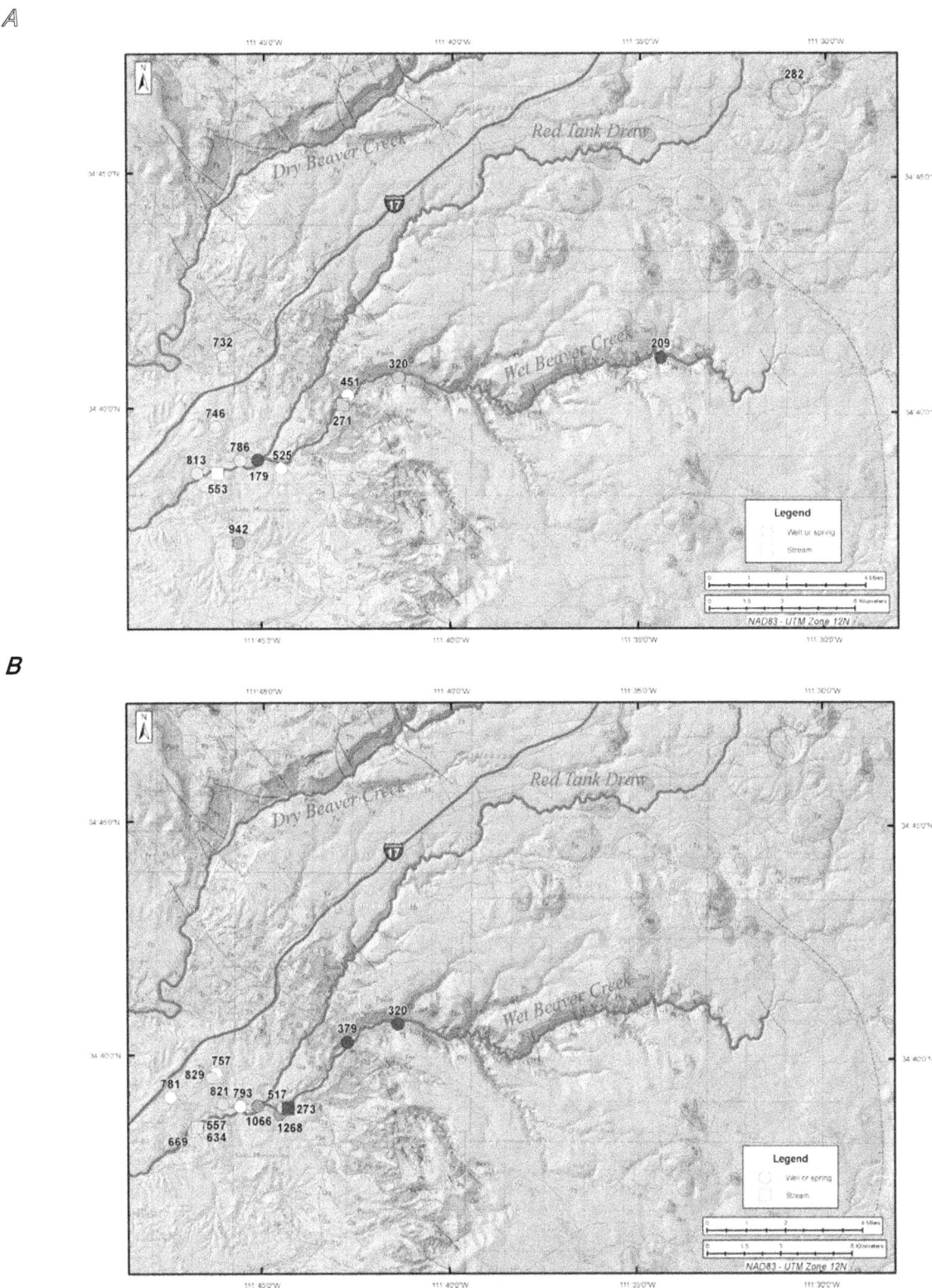

Figure 23. Specific conductance in µS/cm. *A*, 2006 data. *B*, 2008 data.

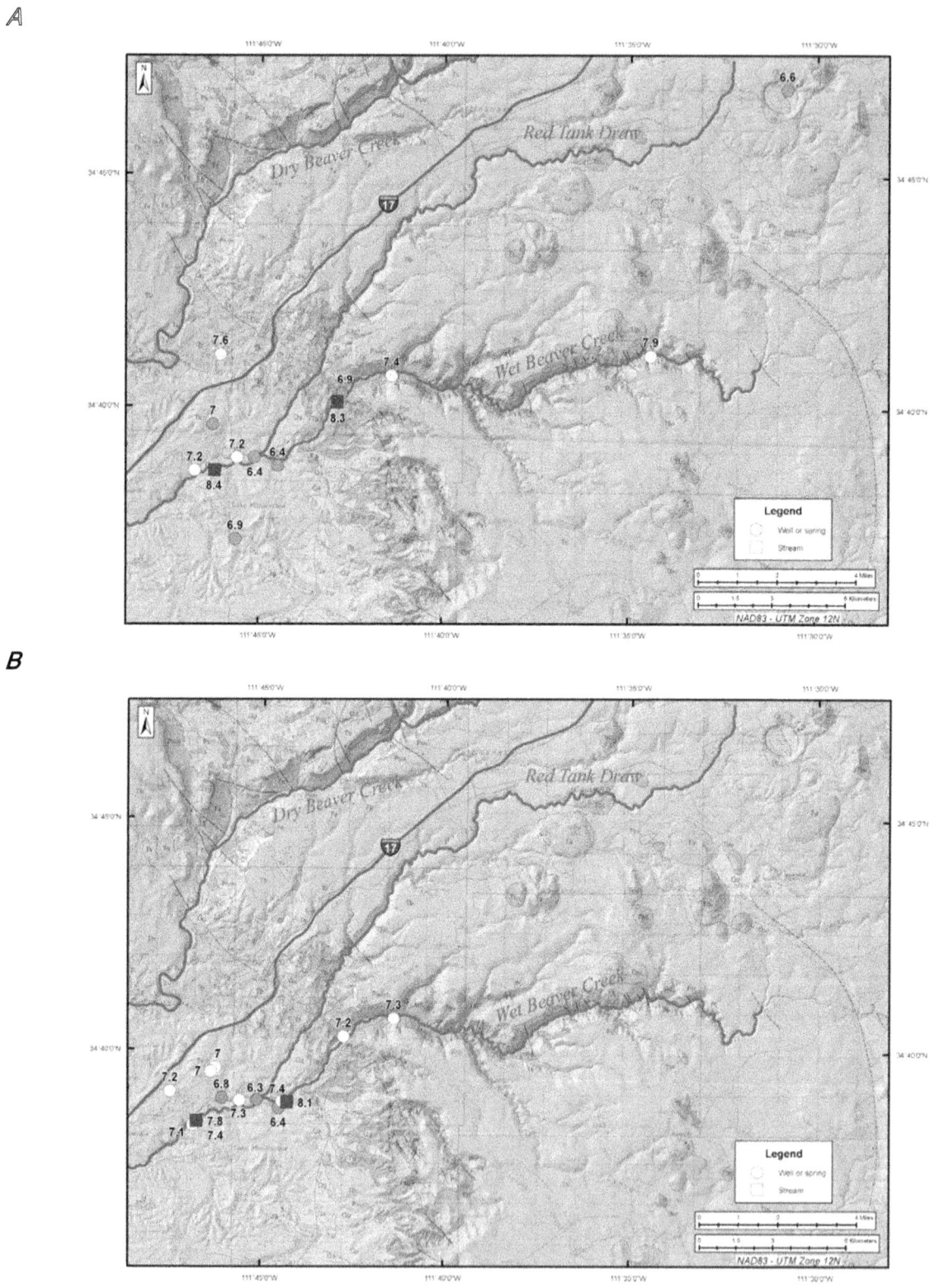

Figure 24. pH. *A*, 2006 data. *B*, 2008 data.

A

B

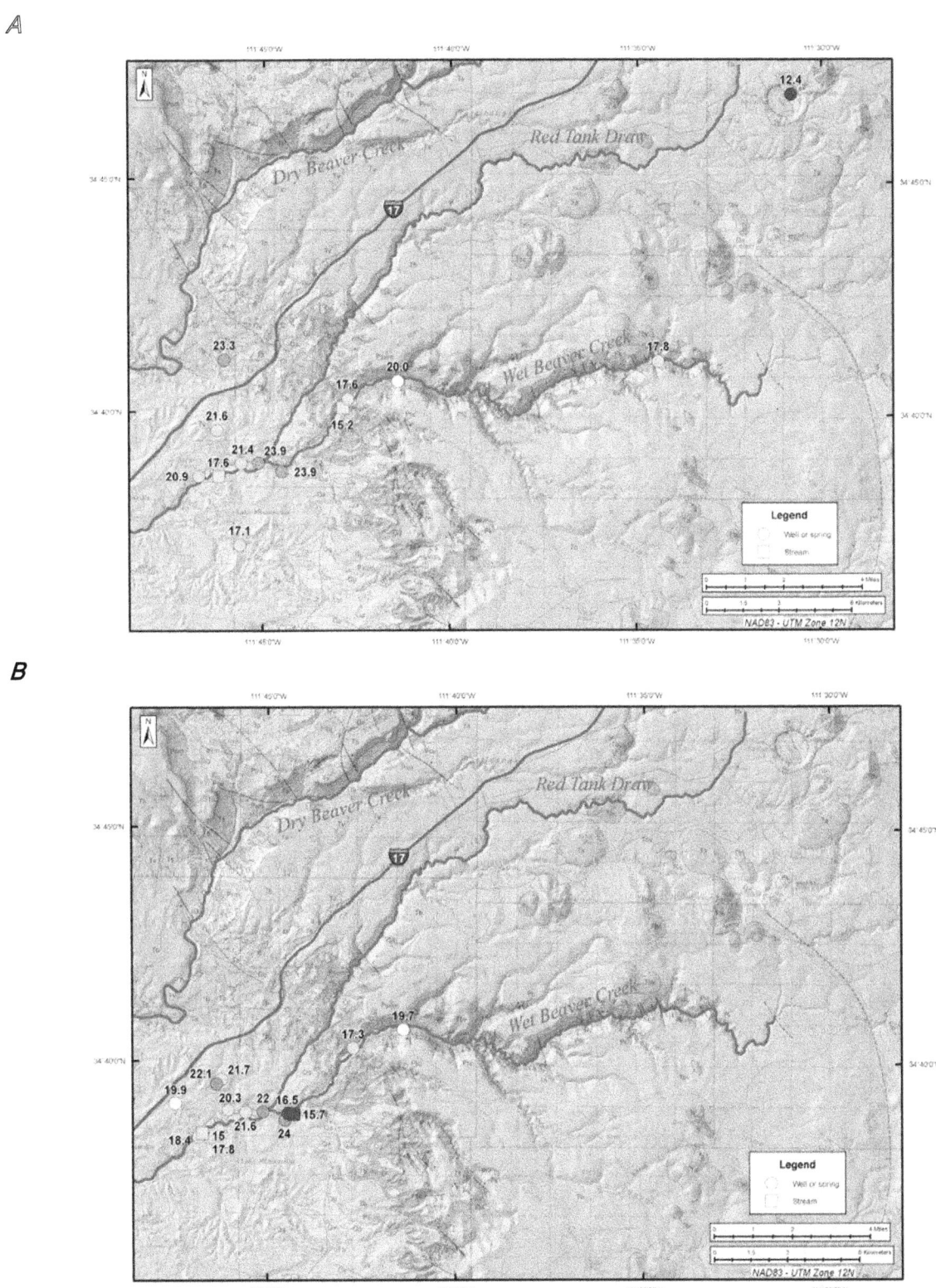

Figure 25. Temperature in °C. *A*, 2006 data. *B*, 2008 data.

A

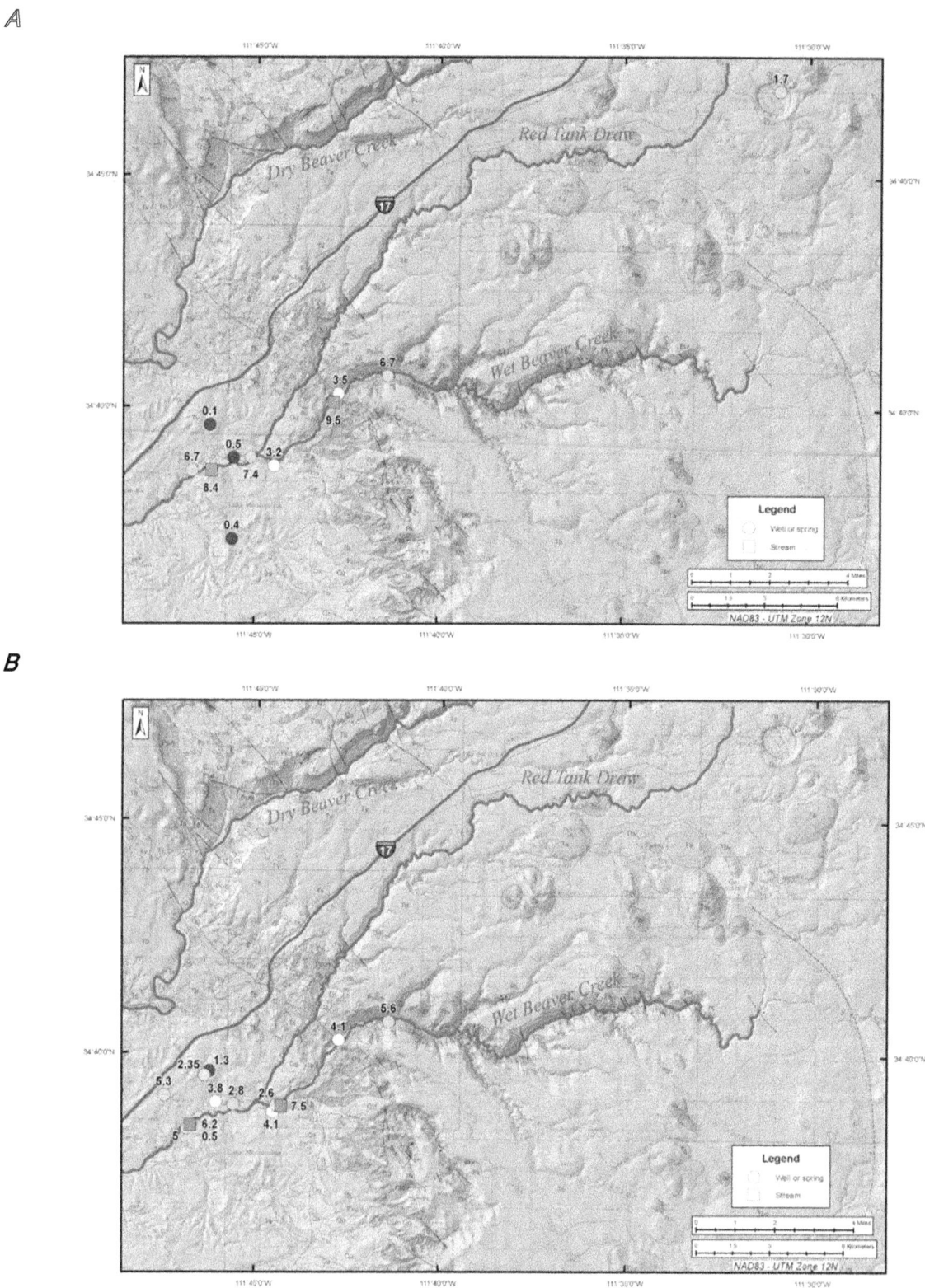

B

Figure 26. Dissolved oxygen in mg/L. *A*, 2006 data. *B*, 2008 data.

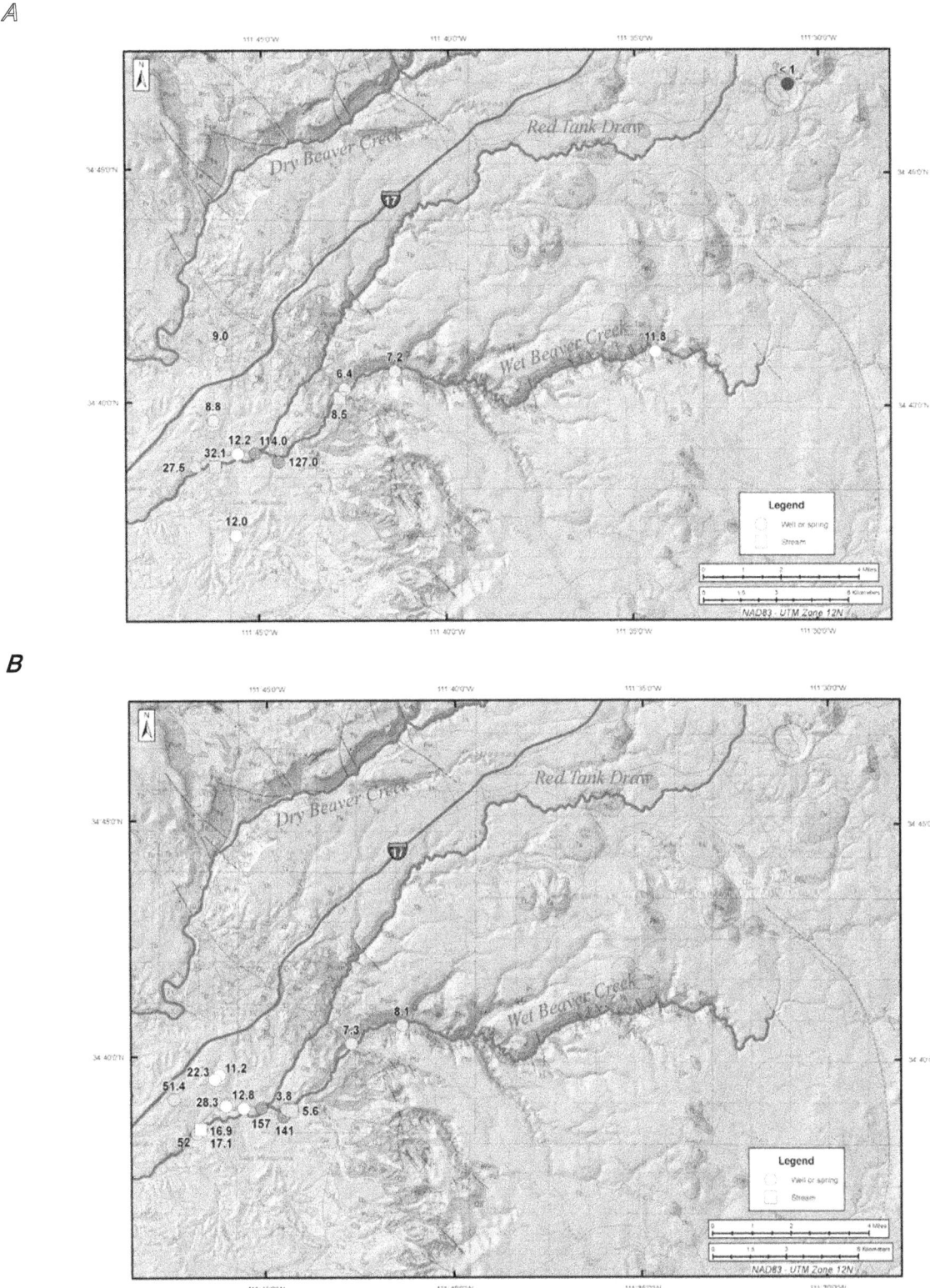

Figure 27. Arsenic in µg/L. *A*, 2006 data. *B*, 2008 data.

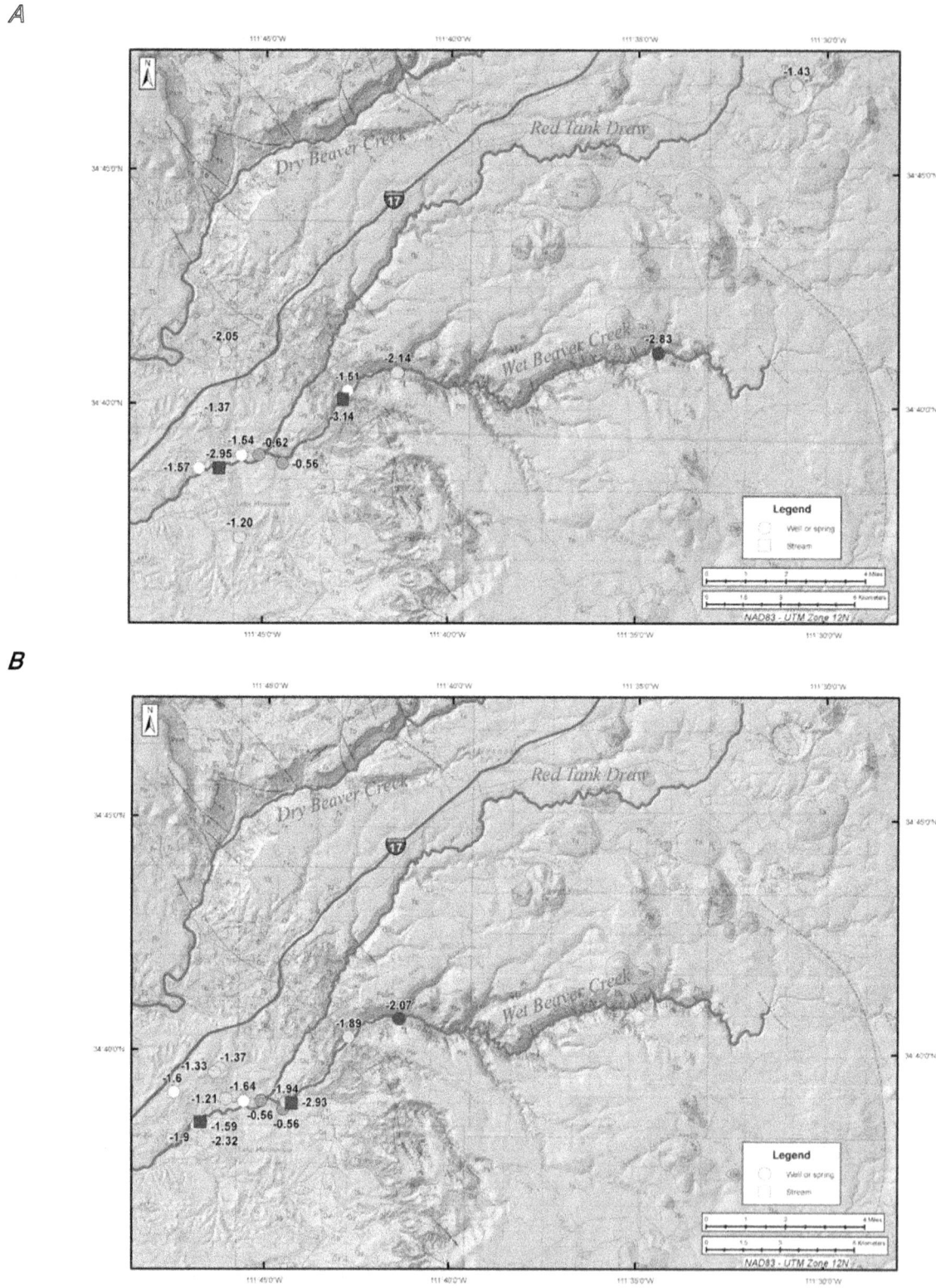

Figure 28. Log partial pressure of carbon dioxide. *A*, 2006 data. *B*, 2008 data.

A

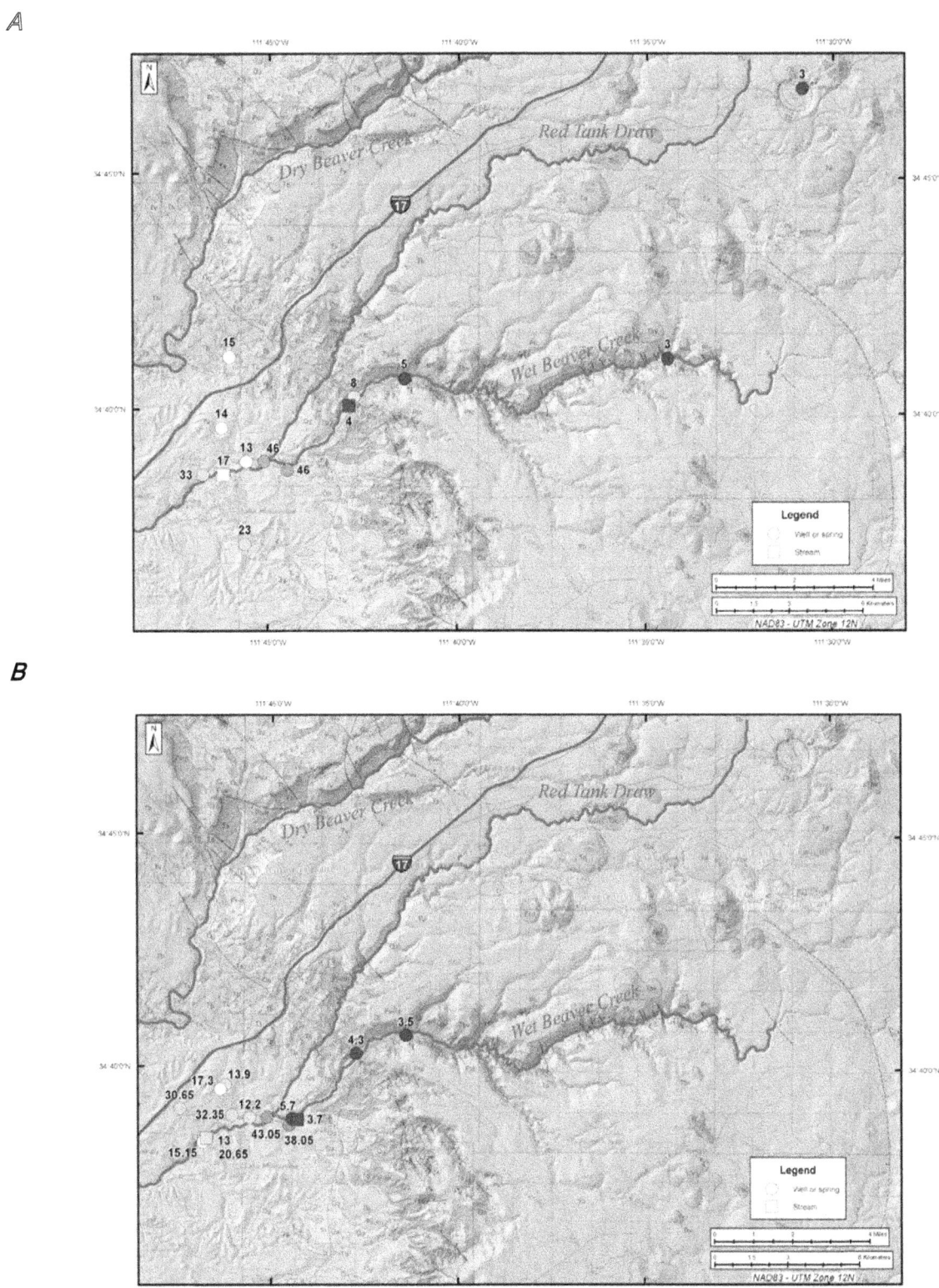

B

Figure 29. Chloride in mg/L. *A*, 2006 data. *B*, 2008 data.

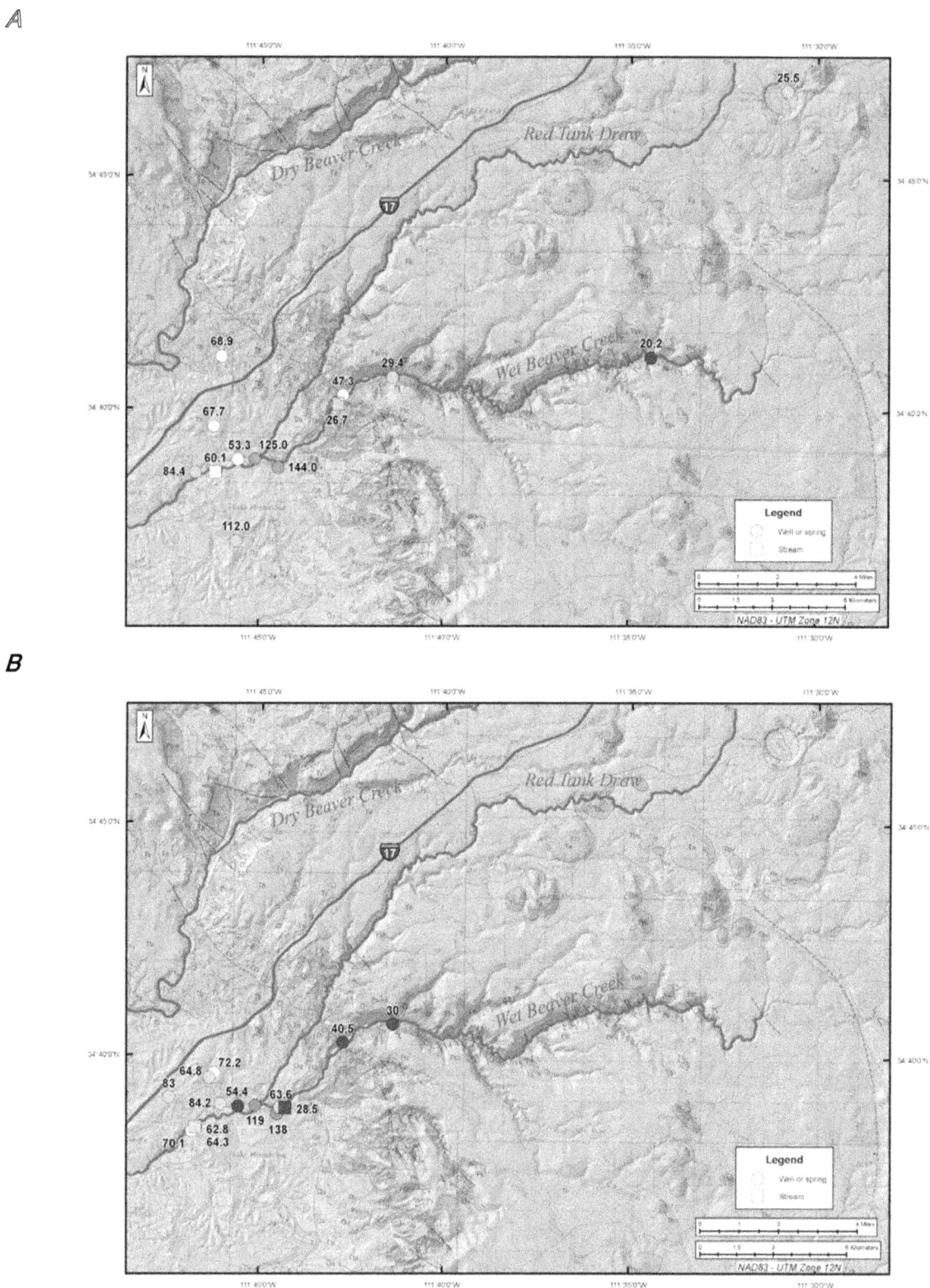

Figure 30. Calcium in mg/L. *A*, 2006 data. *B*, 2008 data.

A

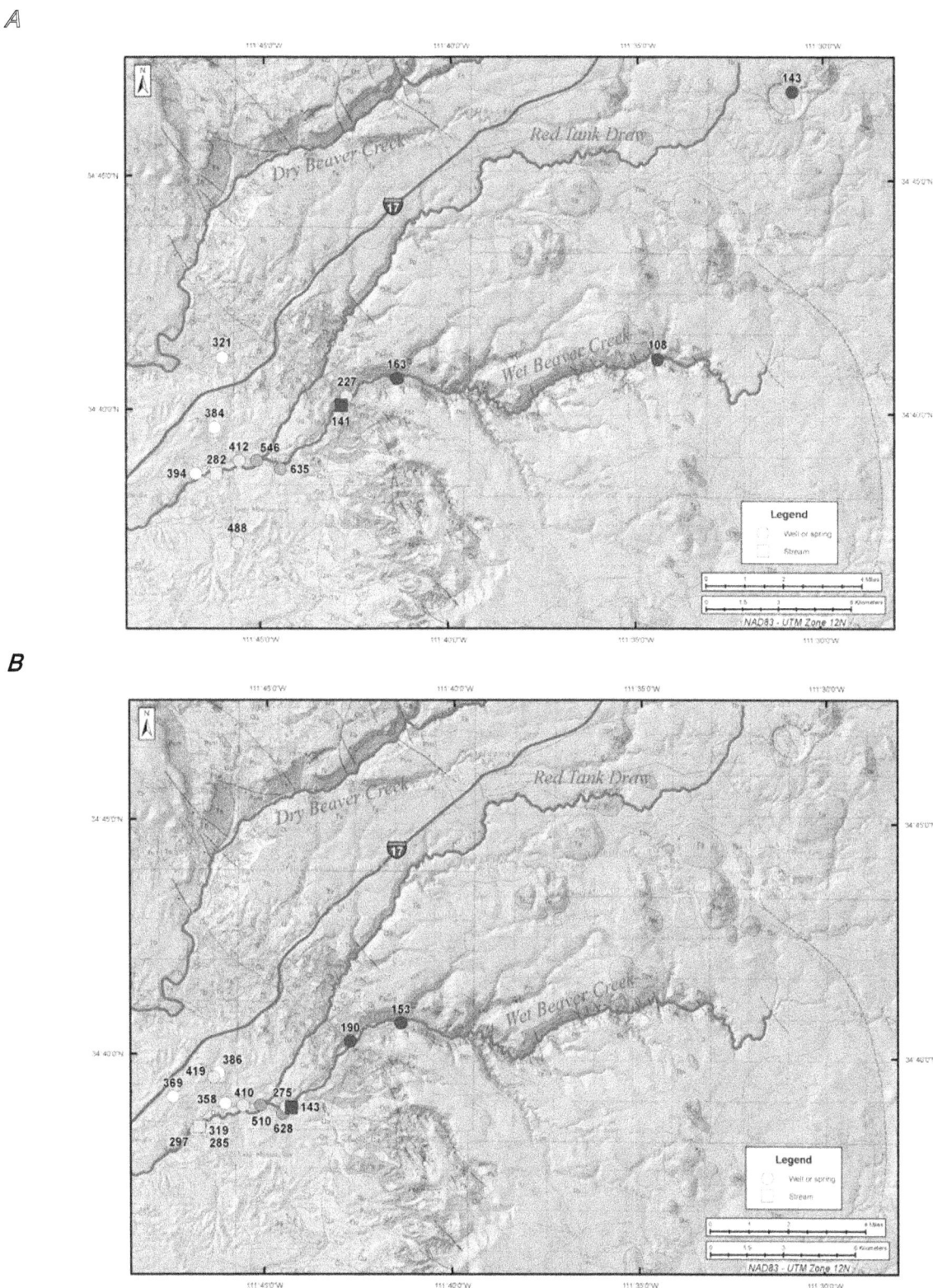

B

Figure 31. Alkalinity as CaCO₃ in mg/L. *A*, 2006 data. *B*, 2008 data.

41

A

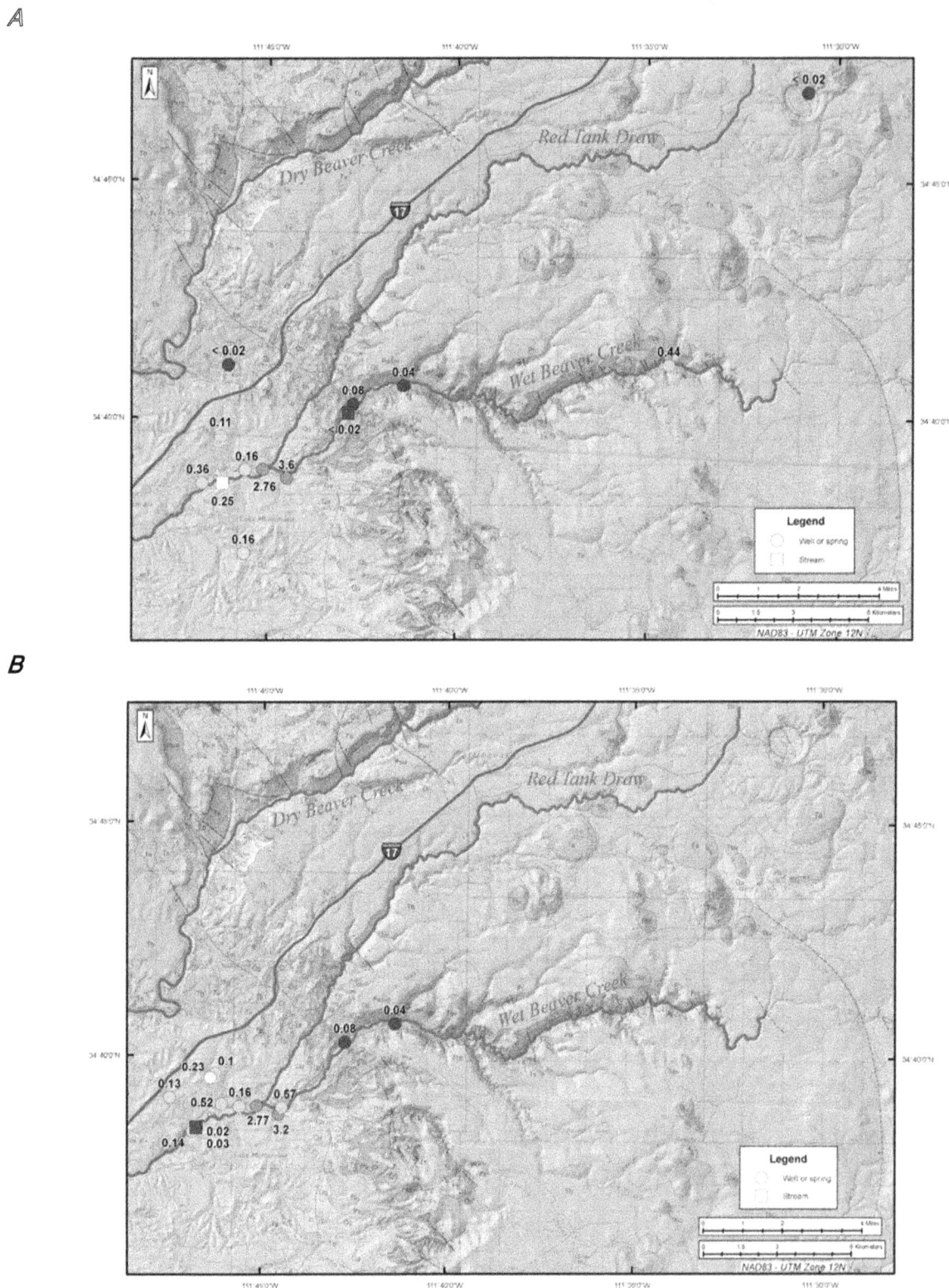

B

Figure 32.   Cesium in µg/L. *A*, 2006 data. *B*, 2008 data.

42

A

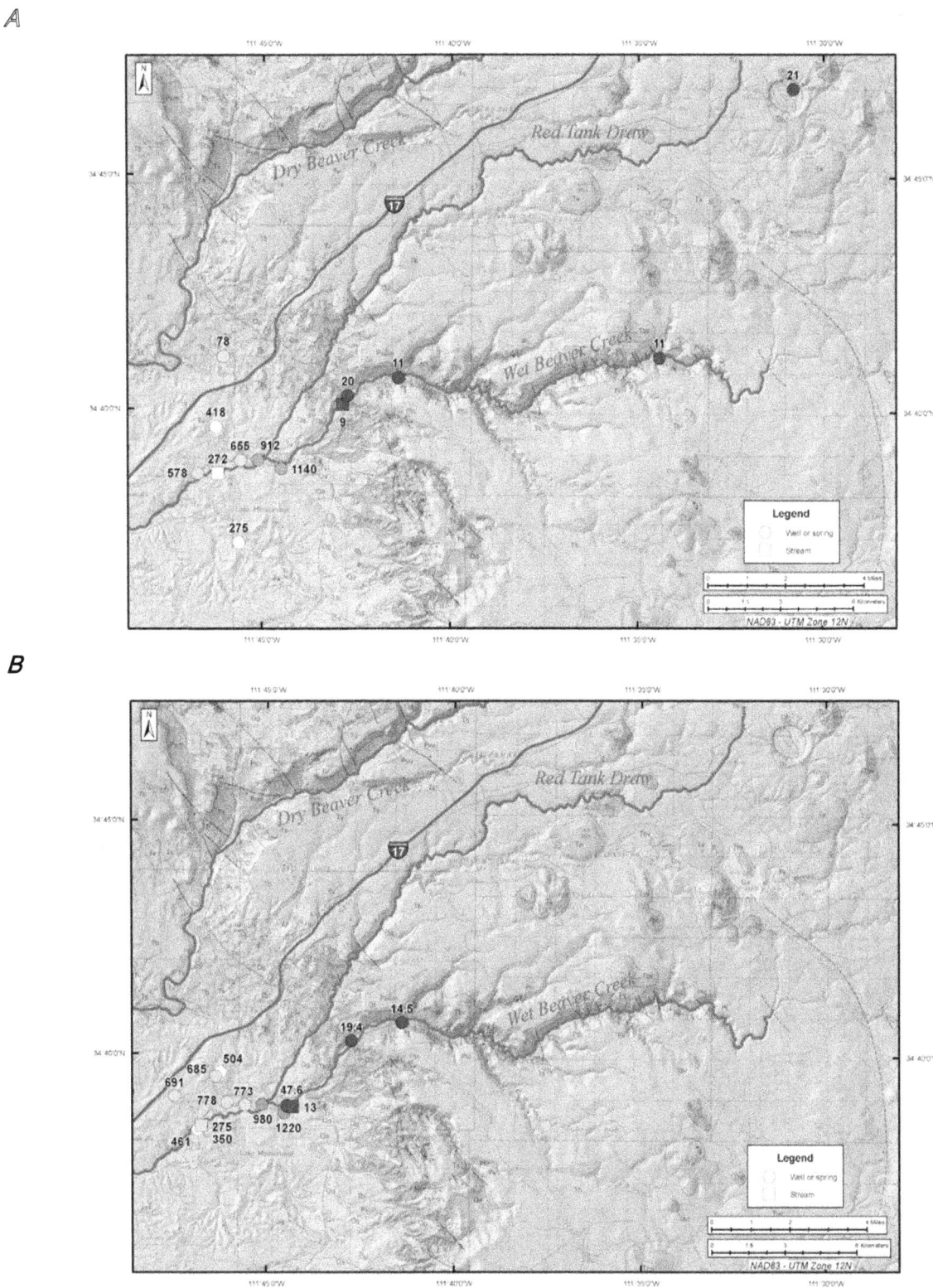

B

Figure 33. Boron in μg/L. *A*, 2006 data. *B*, 2008 data.

43

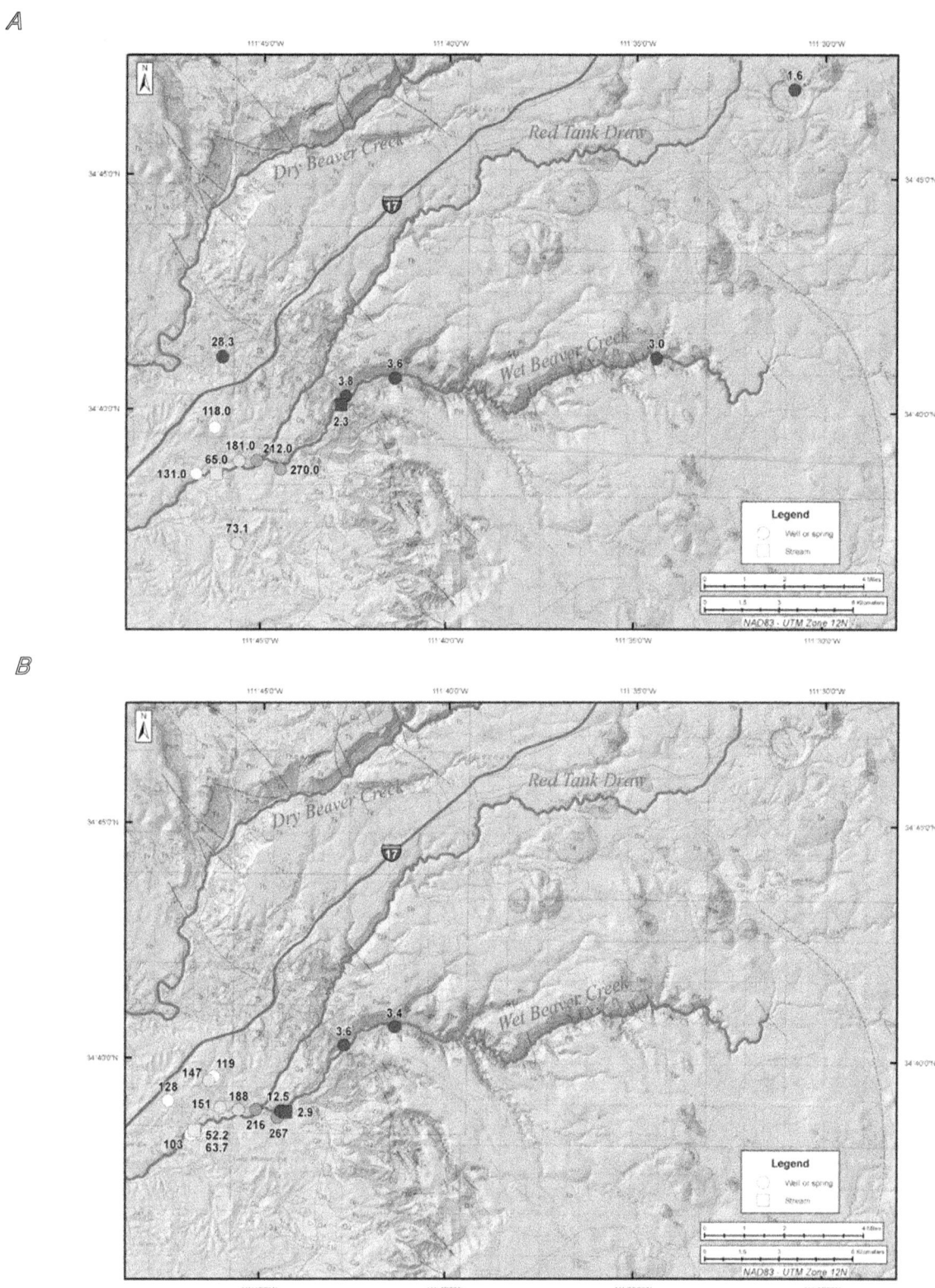

Figure 34. Lithium in µg/L. *A*, 2006 data. *B*, 2008 data.

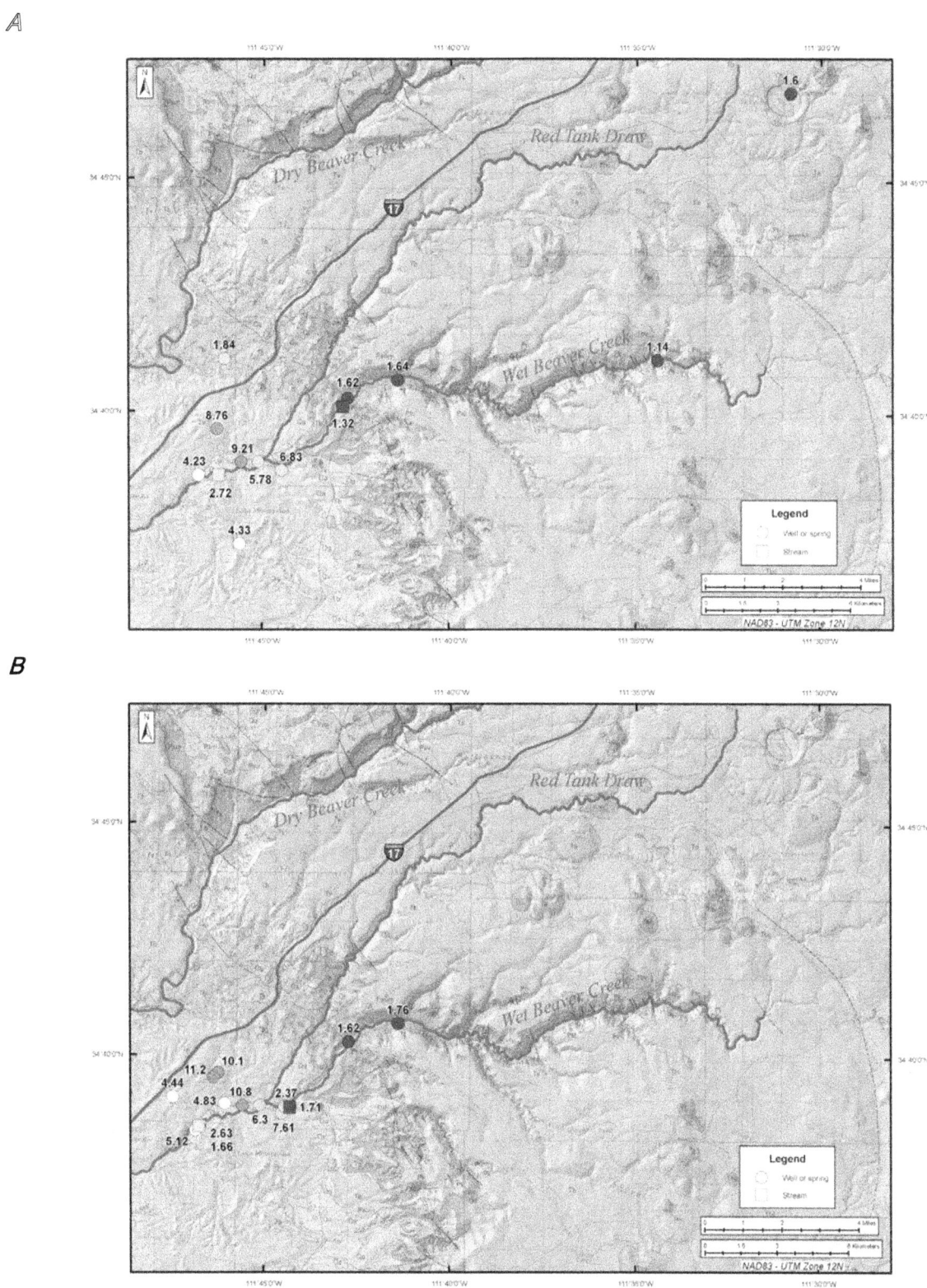

Figure 35. Potassium in mg/L. *A*, 2006 data. *B*, 2008 data.

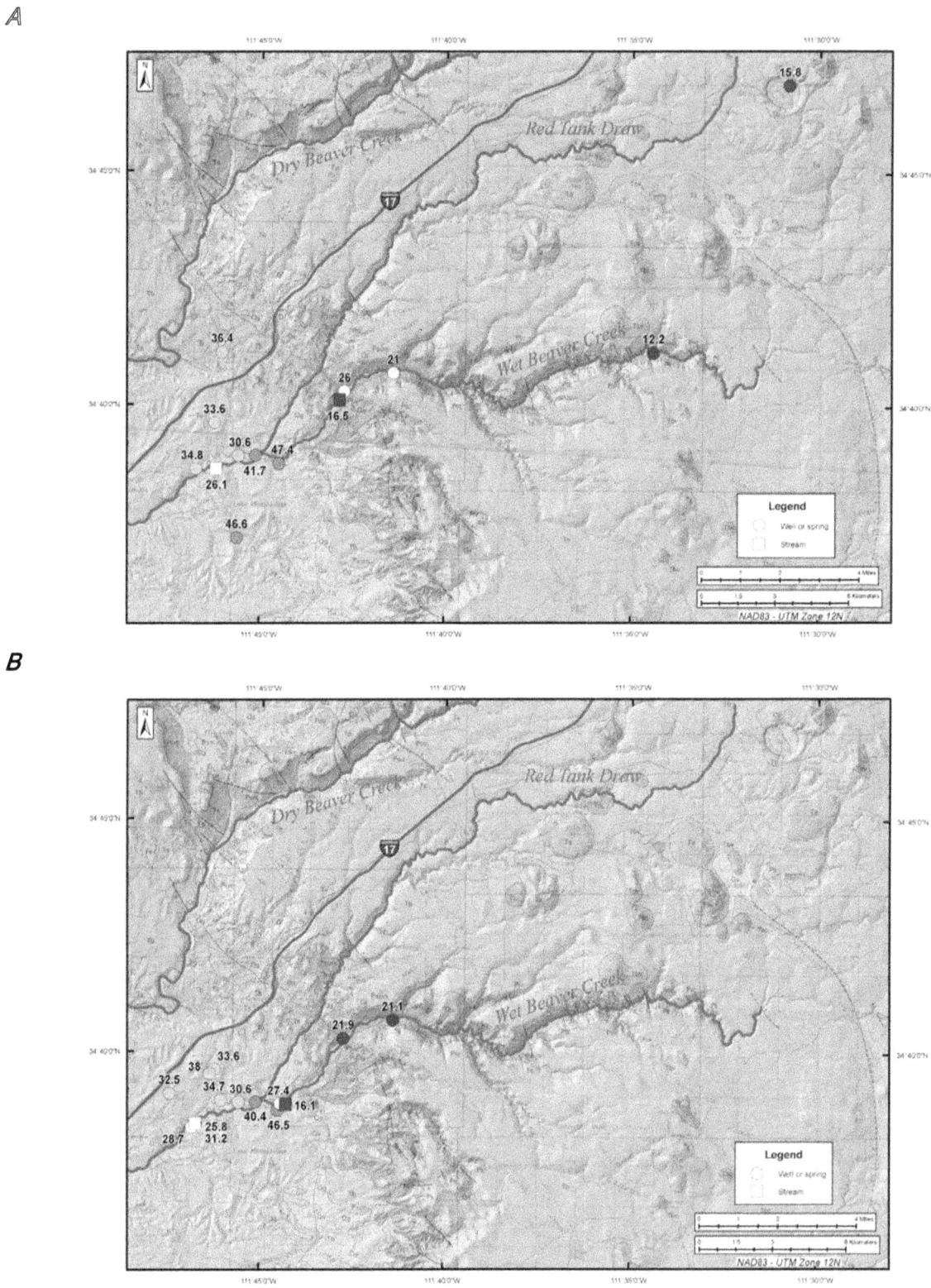

Figure 36. Magnesium in mg/L. *A*, 2006 data. *B*, 2008 data.

_A_

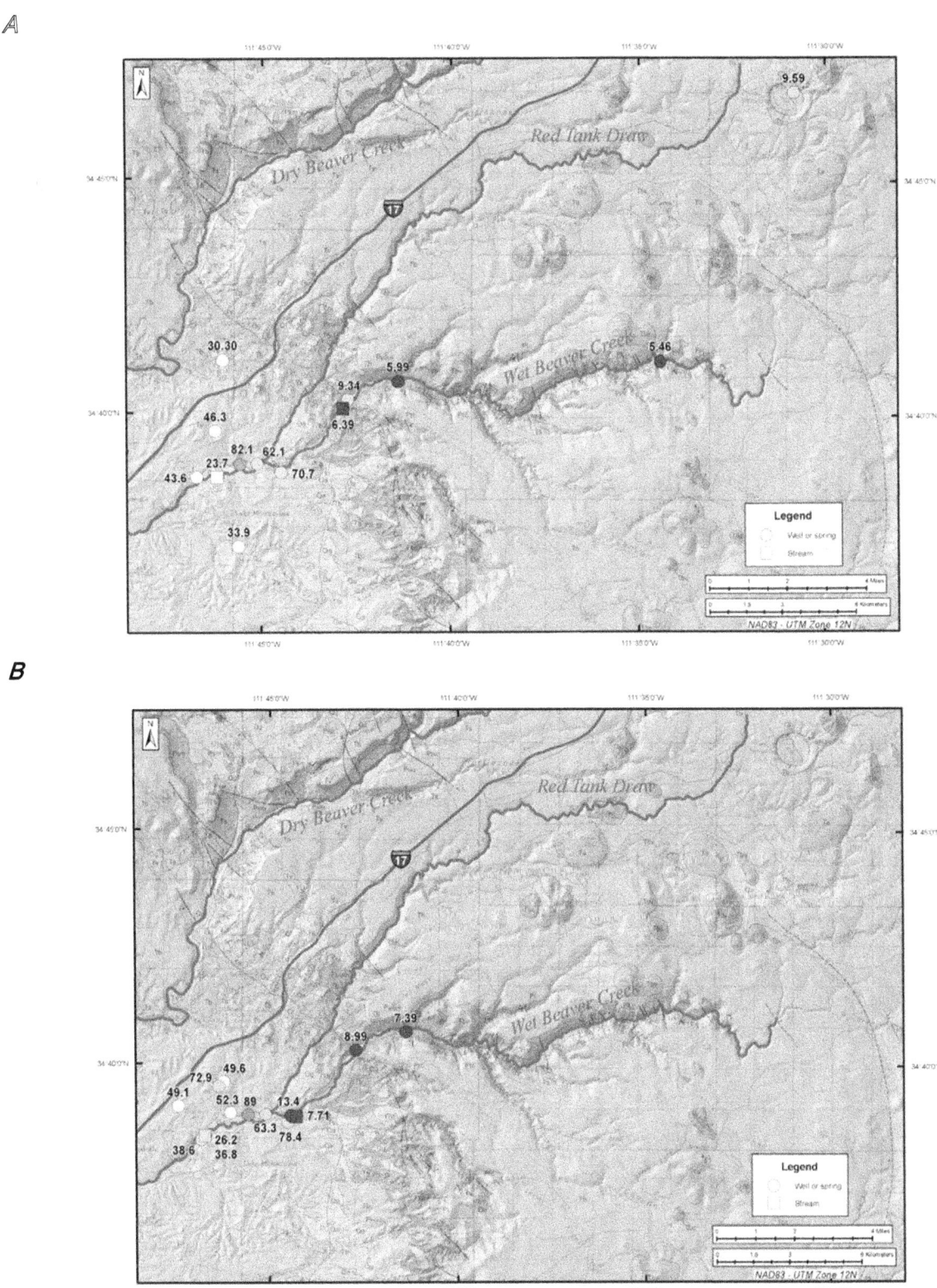

Figure 37. Sodium in mg/L. _A_, 2006 data. _B_, 2008 data.

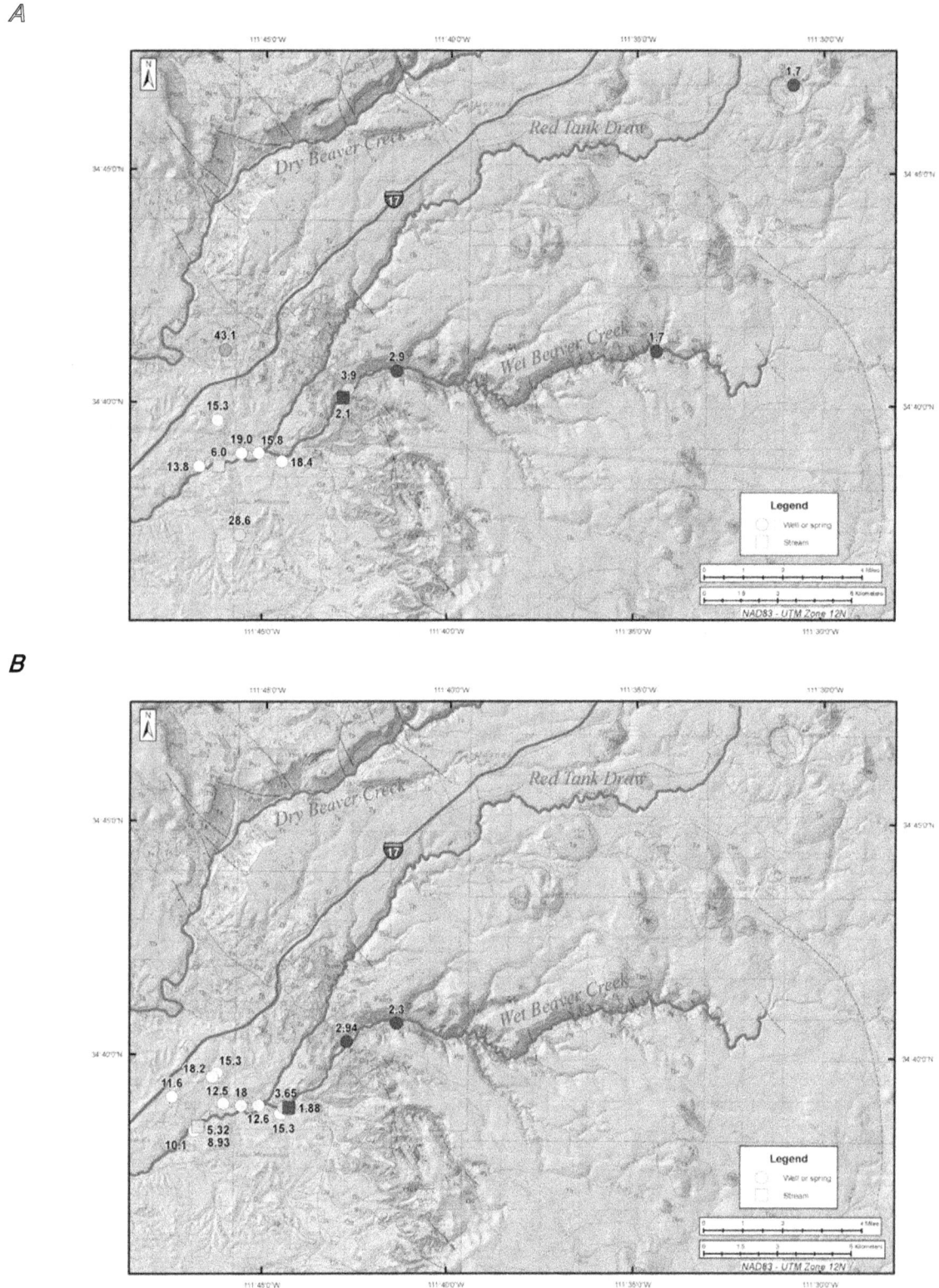

Figure 38. Sulfate in mg/L. *A*, 2006 data. *B*, 2008 data.

A

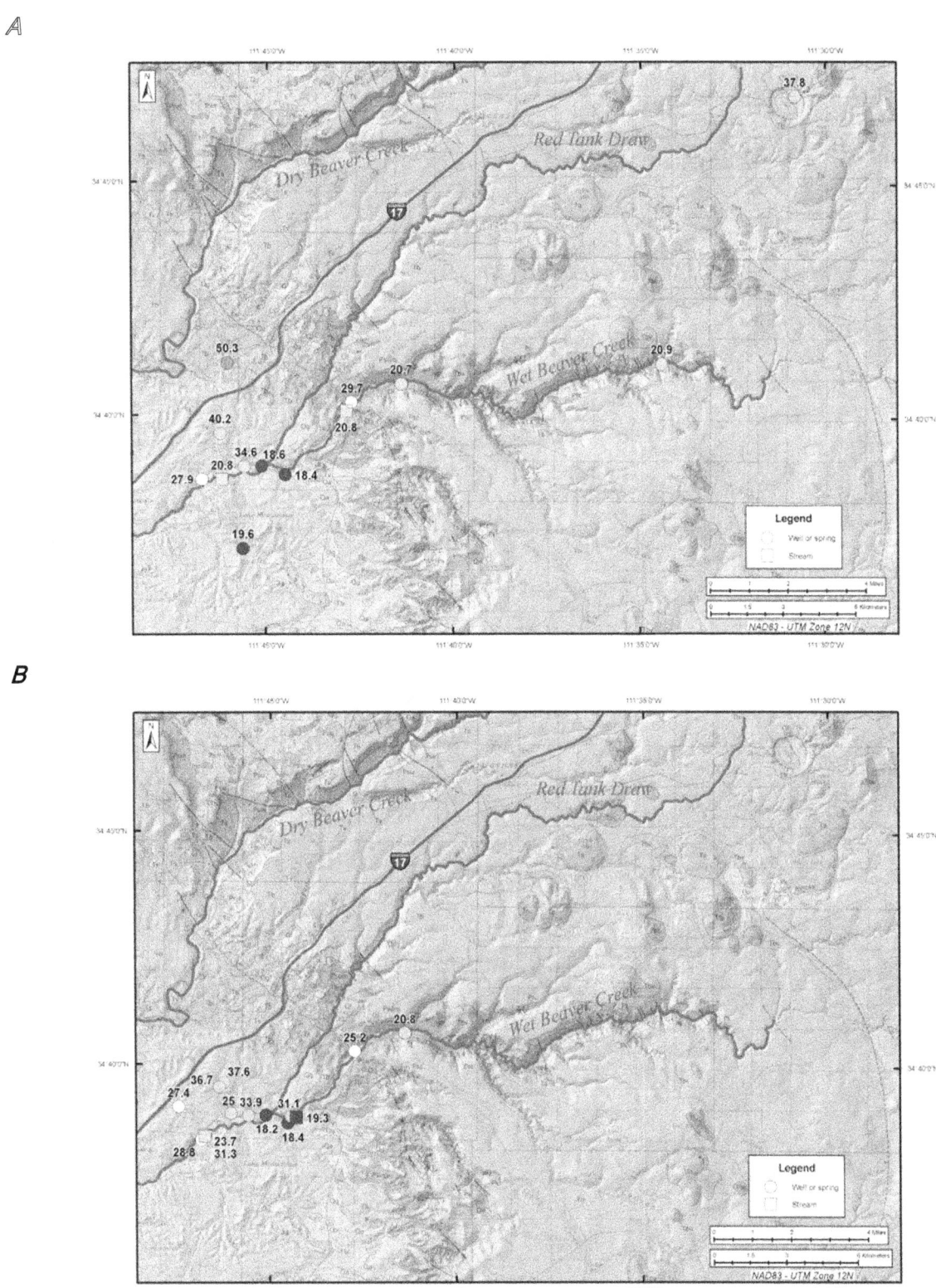

B

Figure 39. Silica in mg/L. *A*, 2006 data. *B*, 2008 data.

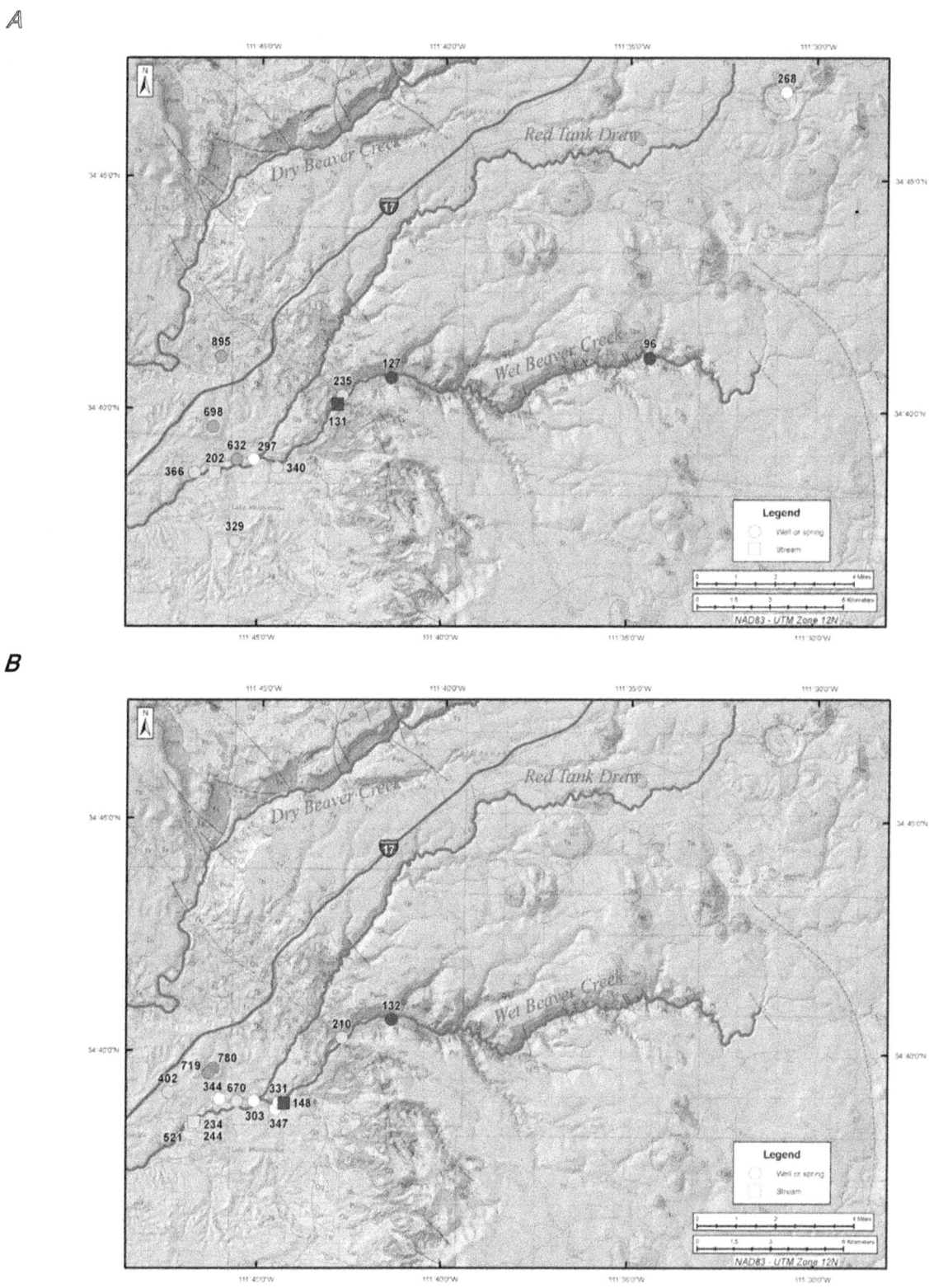

Figure 40. Strontium in μg/L. *A*, 2006 data. *B*, 2008 data.

A

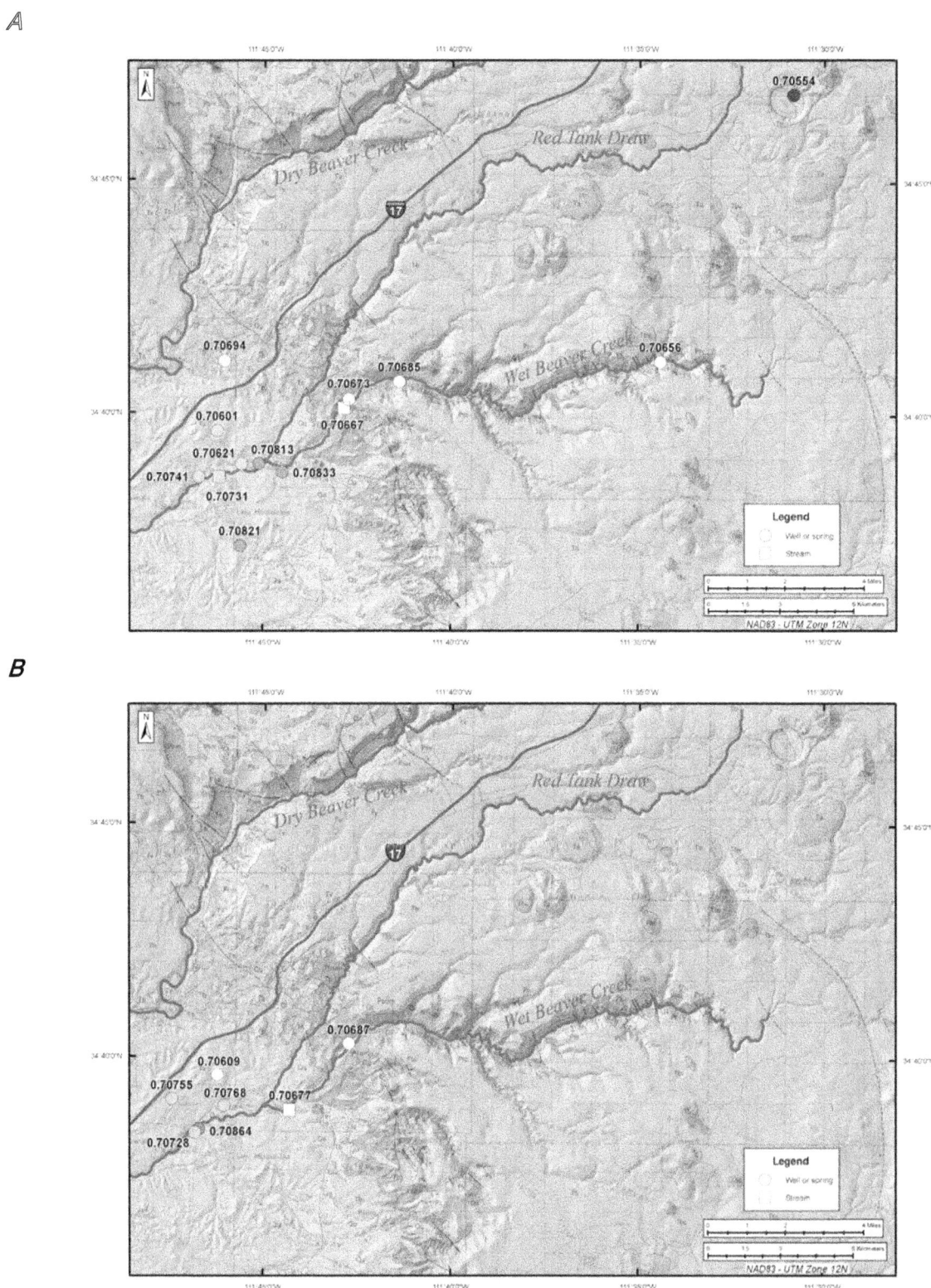

B

Figure 41. $^{87}Sr/^{86}Sr$ (strontium). *A*, 2006 data. *B*, 2008 data.

51

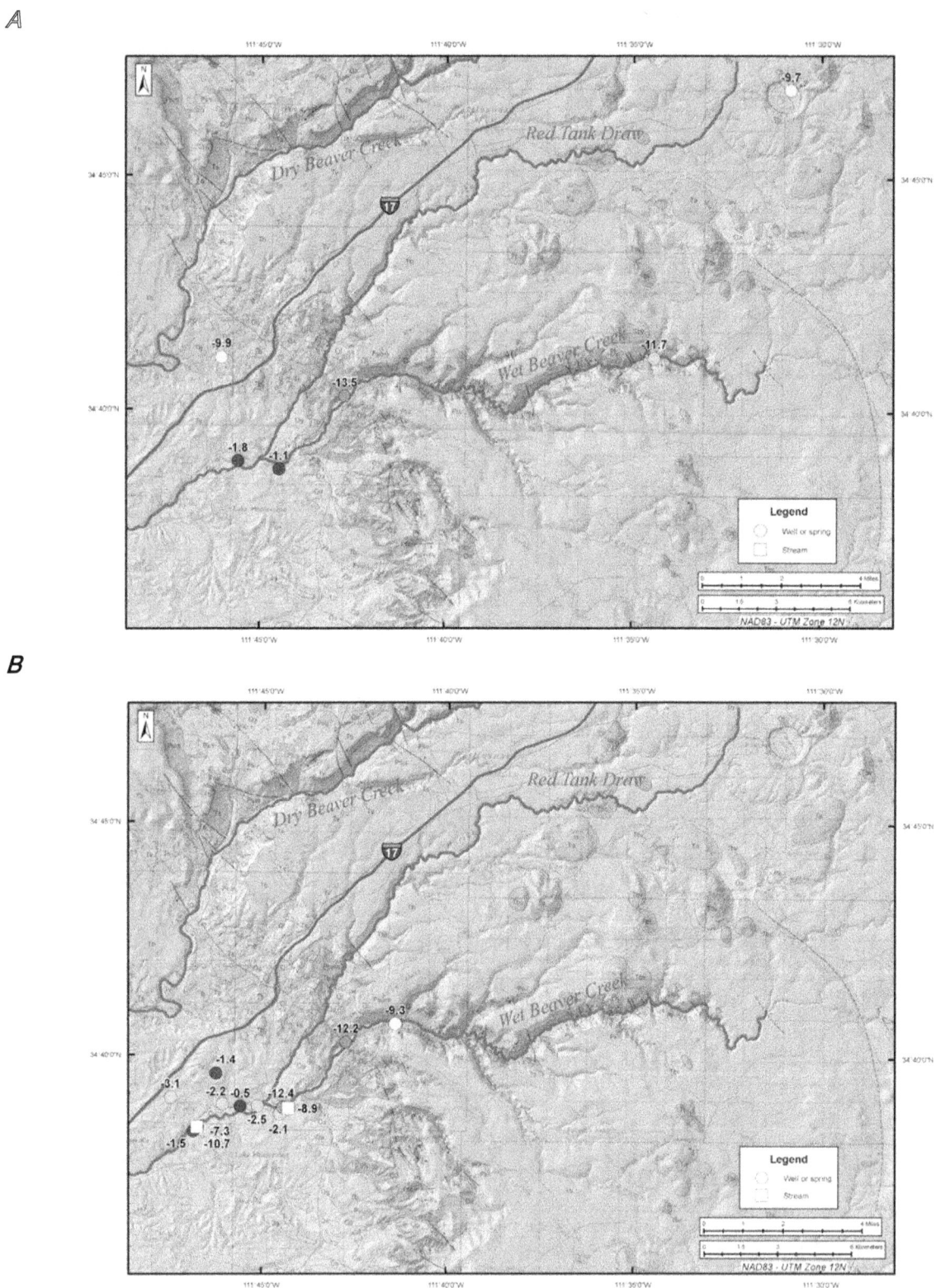

Figure 42. δ¹³C ‰. *A*, 2006 data. *B*, 2008 data.

A

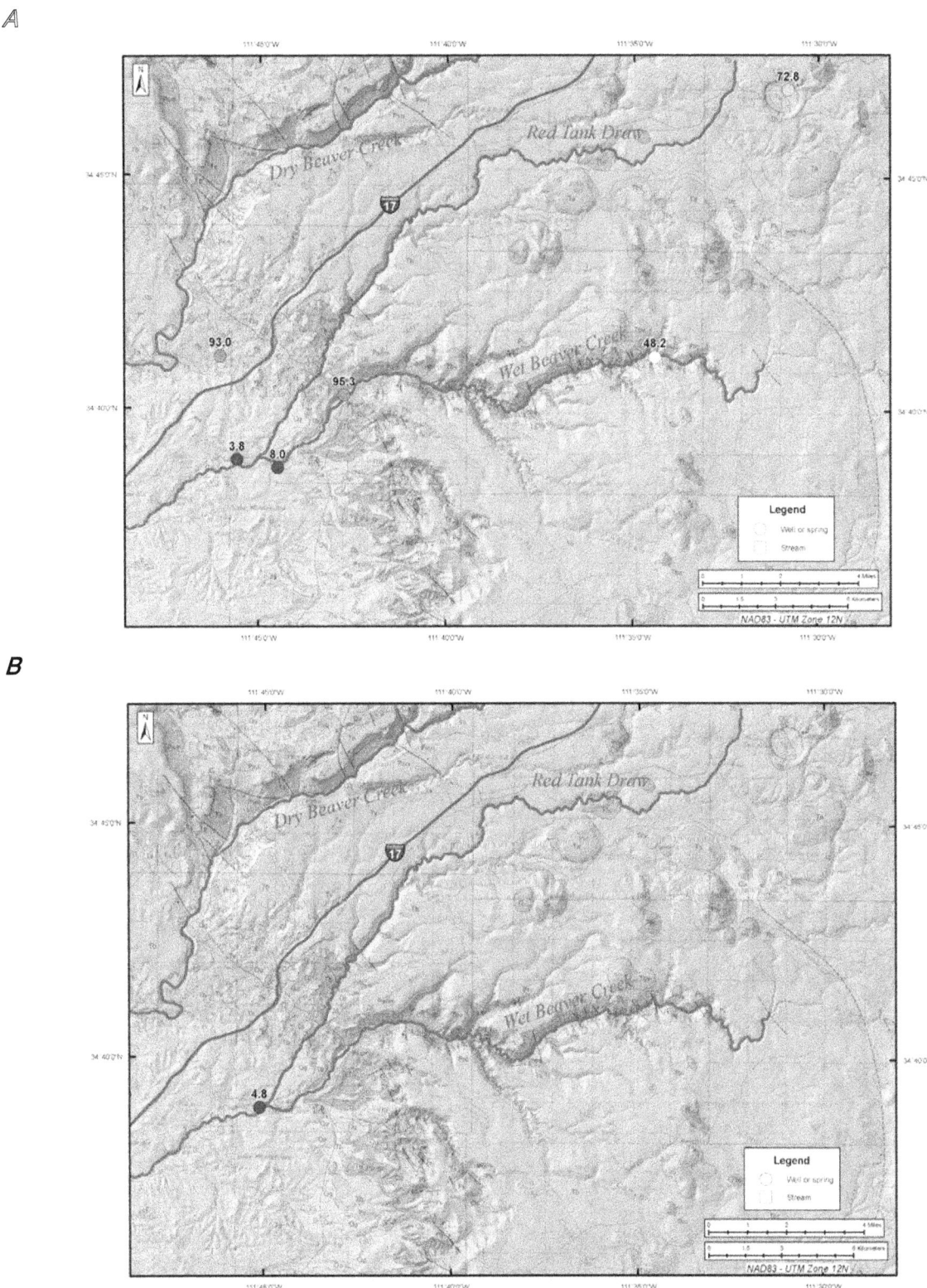

B

Figure 43. ^{14}C as percent modern carbon. *A*, 2006 data. *B*, 2008 data.

A

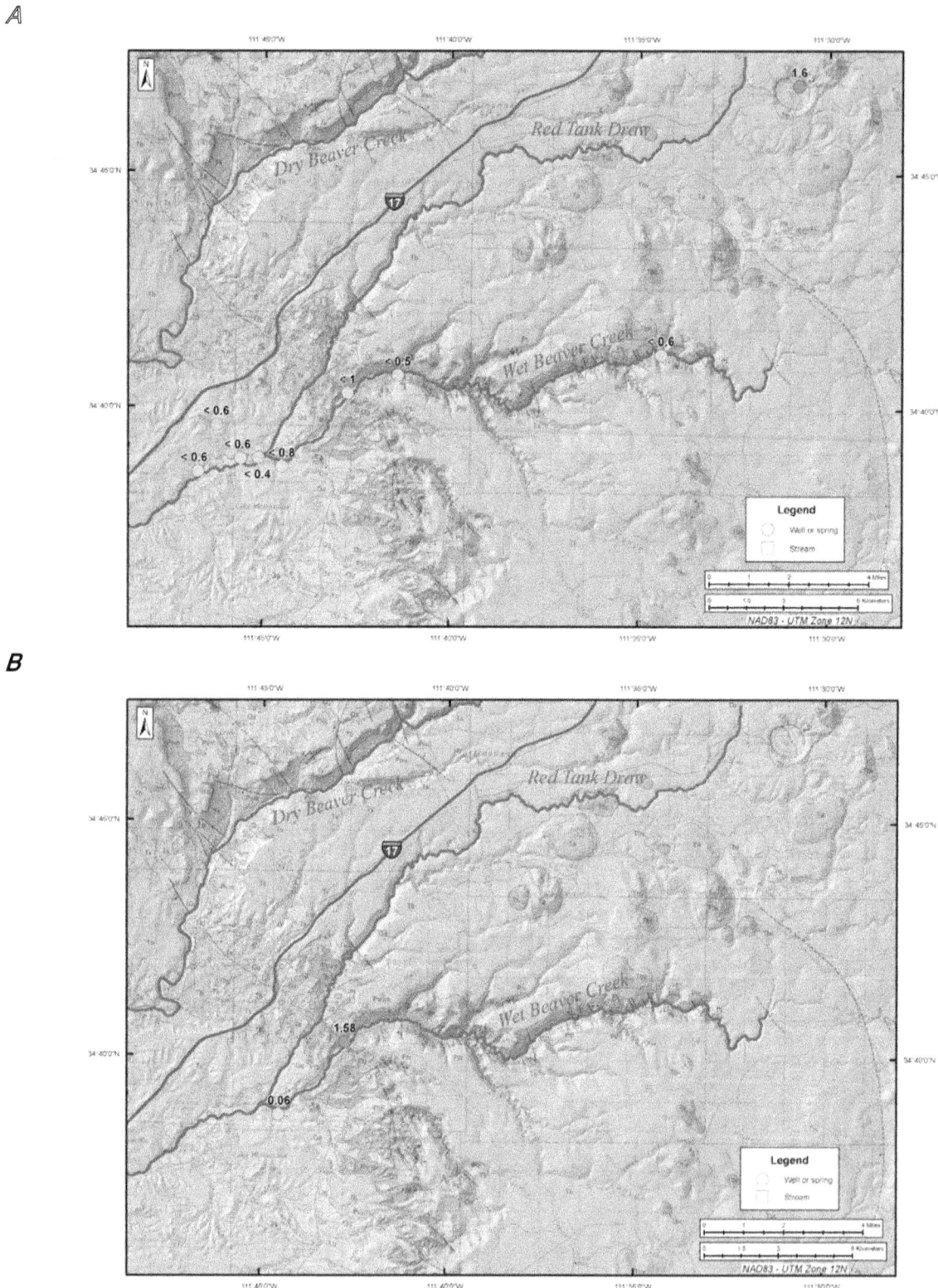

B

Figure 44. Tritium reported in tritium units. *A*, 2006 data. *B*, 2008 data.

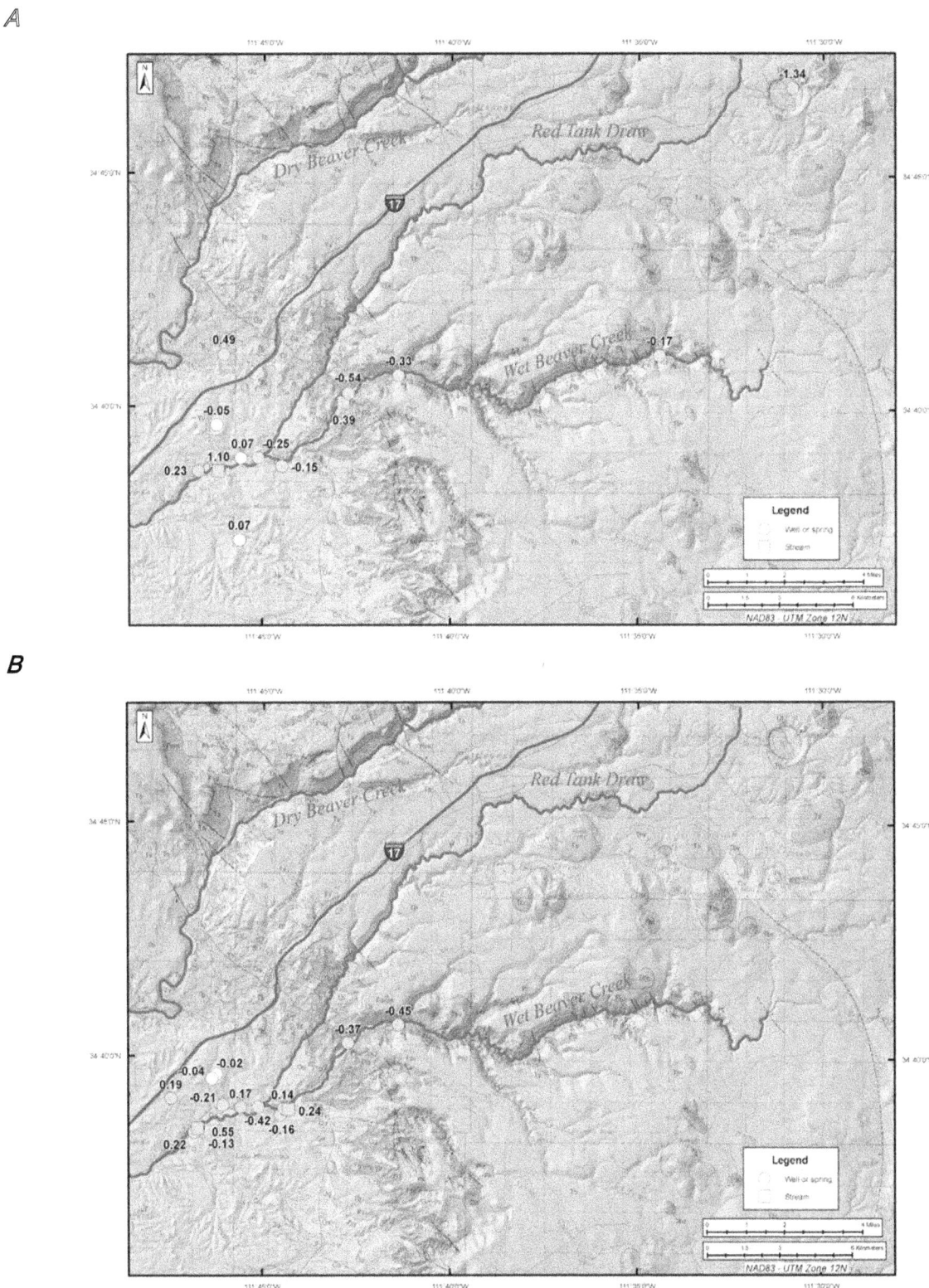

Figure 45. Calcite saturation index. *A*, 2006 data. *B*, 2008 data.

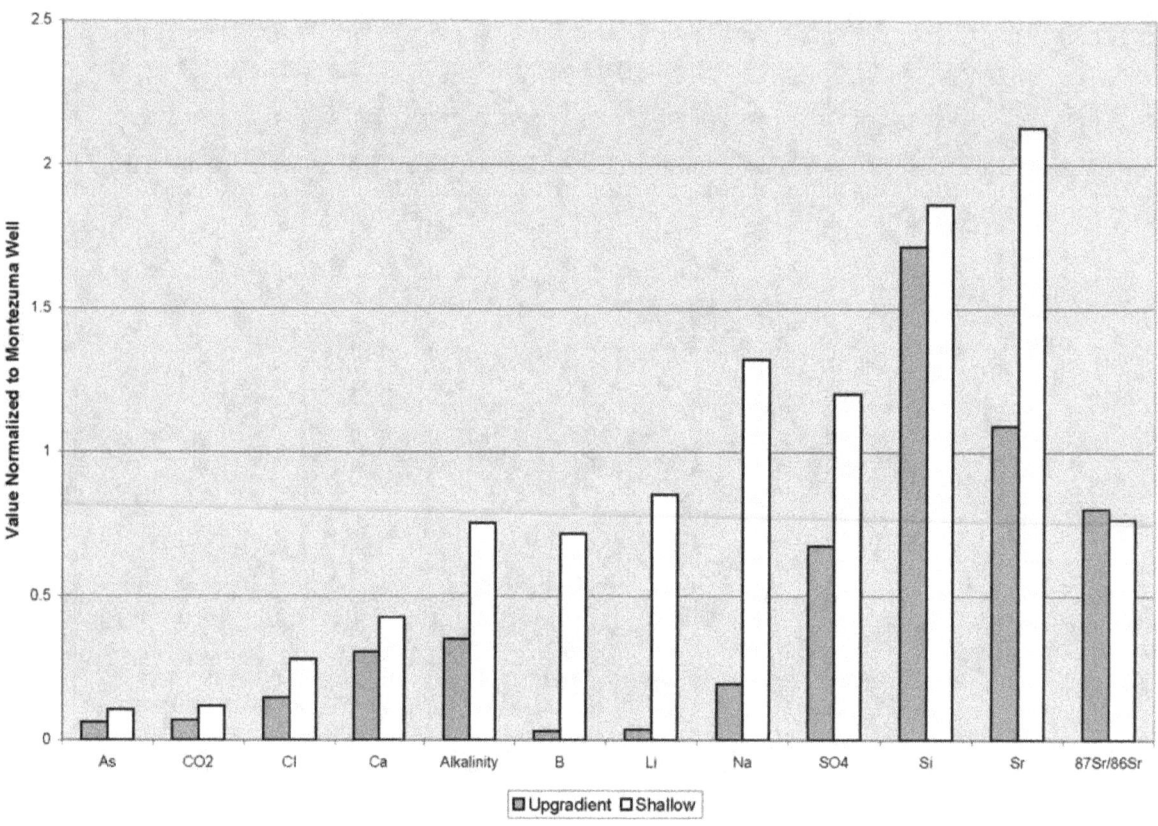

Figure 46. Selected constituents normalized to Montezuma Well with upgradient and shallow zones.

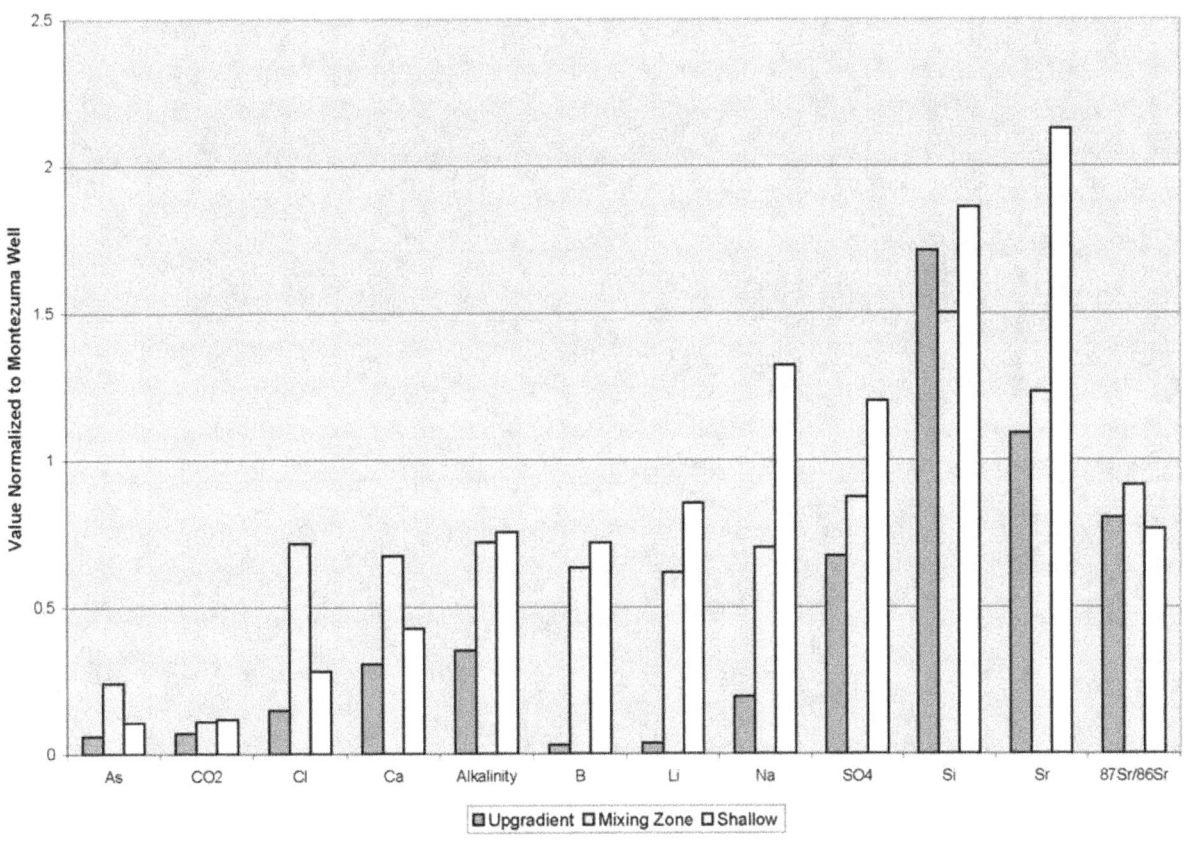

Figure 47. Selected constituents normalized to Montezuma Well with upgradient, mixing, and shallow zones.

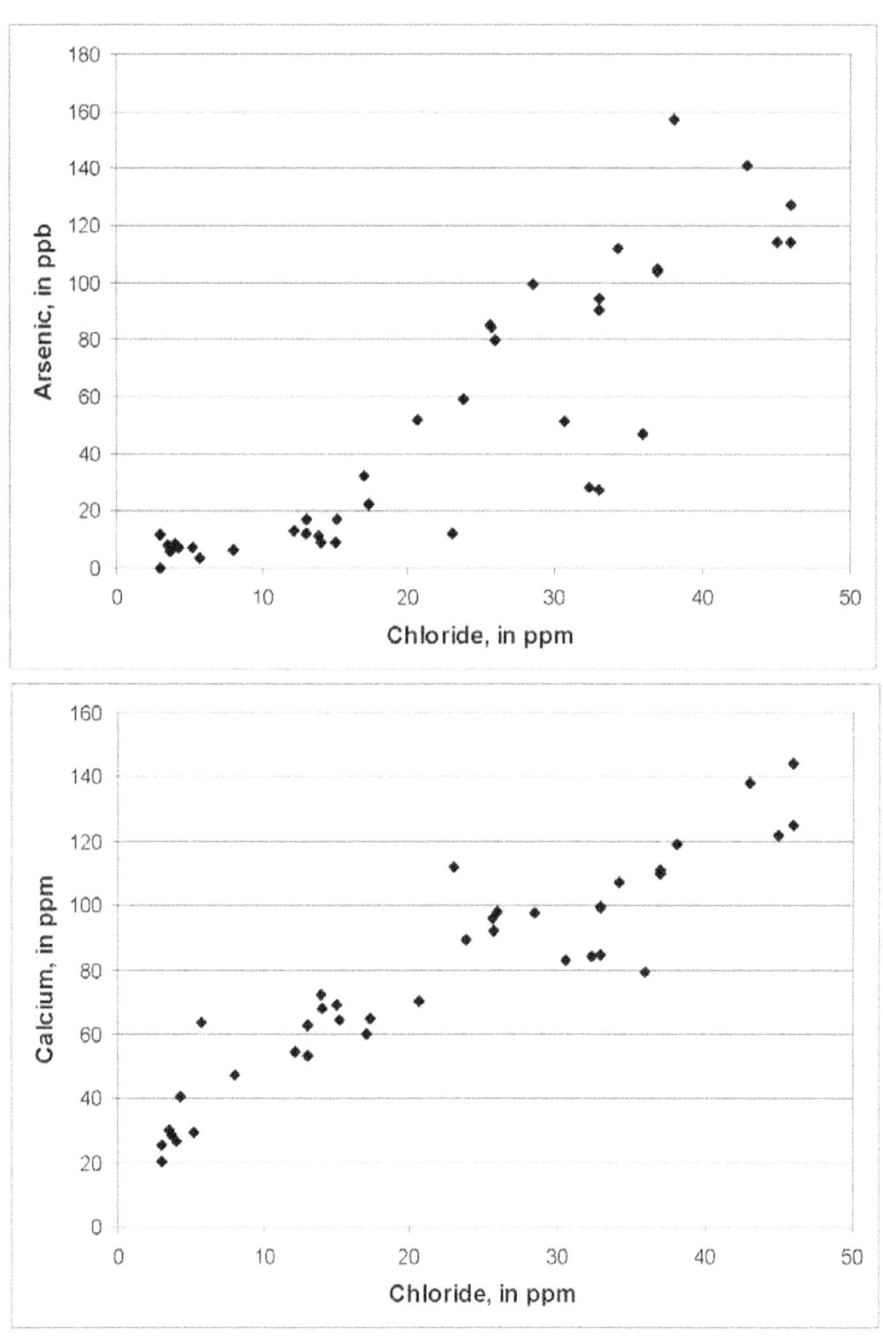

Figure 48. Arsenic and calcium concentrations compared to chloride concentrations for all water samples.

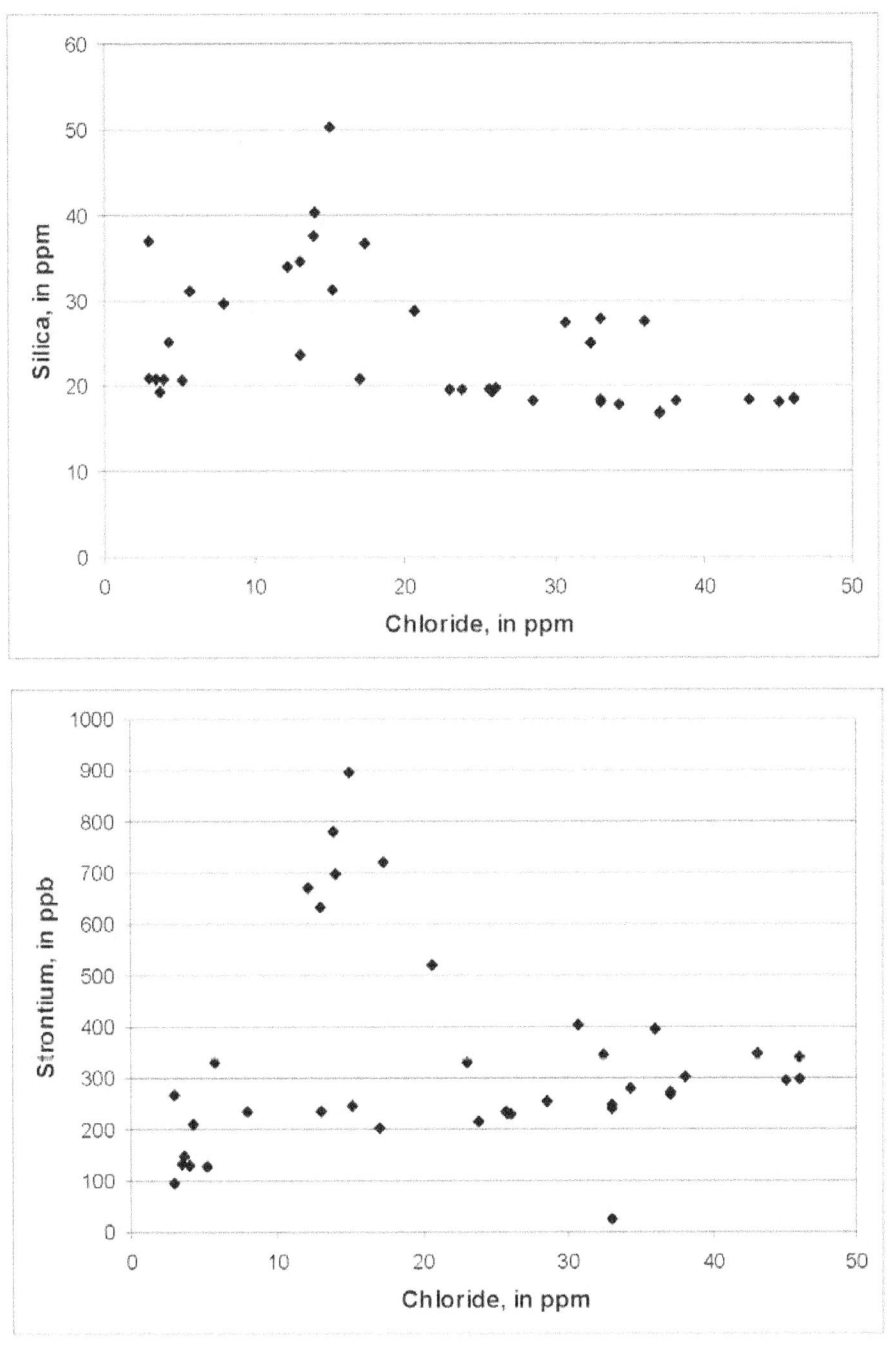

Figure 49. Silica and strontium concentrations compared to chloride concentrations for all water samples.

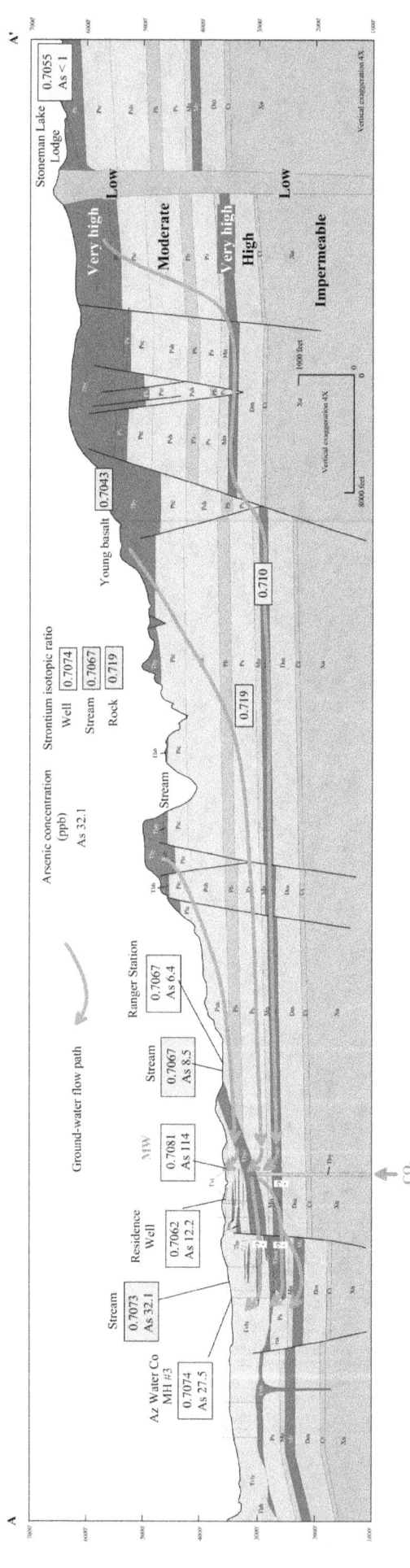

Figure 50. Groundwater flow paths and strontium isotopic ratios in surface waters and wells.

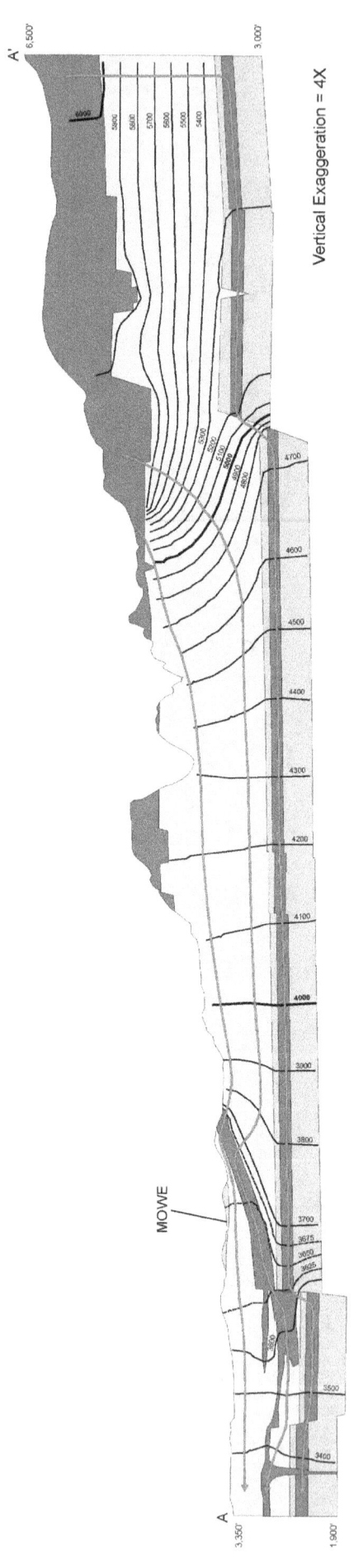

Red lines = ground water flow paths.

Black lines = equipotential hydraulic heads.

Figure 51. Hydraulic heads and flow lines with no basalt dike.

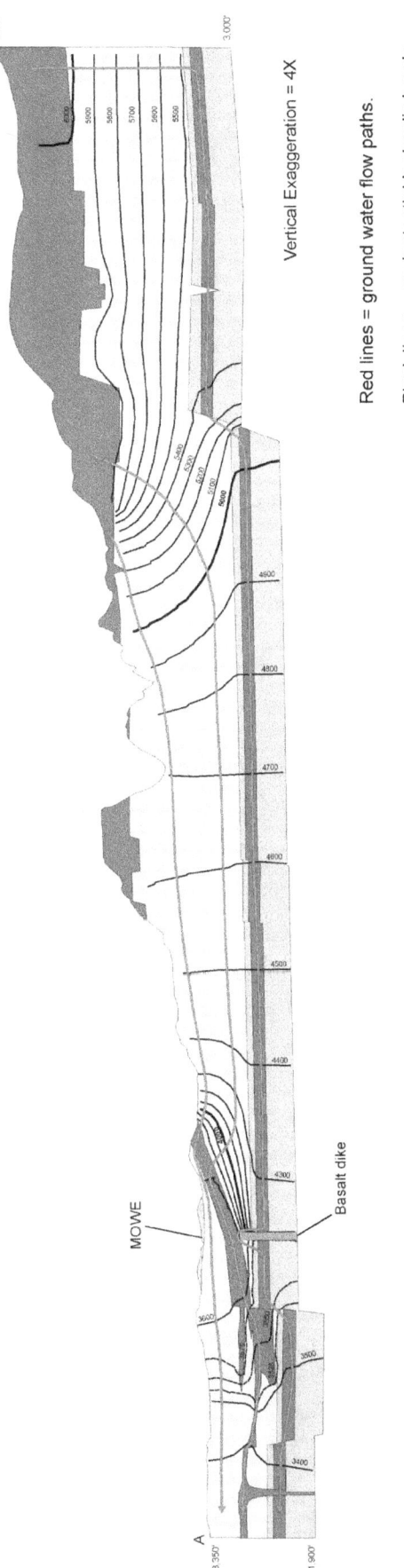

Vertical Exaggeration = 4X

Red lines = ground water flow paths.

Black lines = equipotential hydraulic heads.

Figure 52. Hydraulic heads and flow lines with basalt dike.

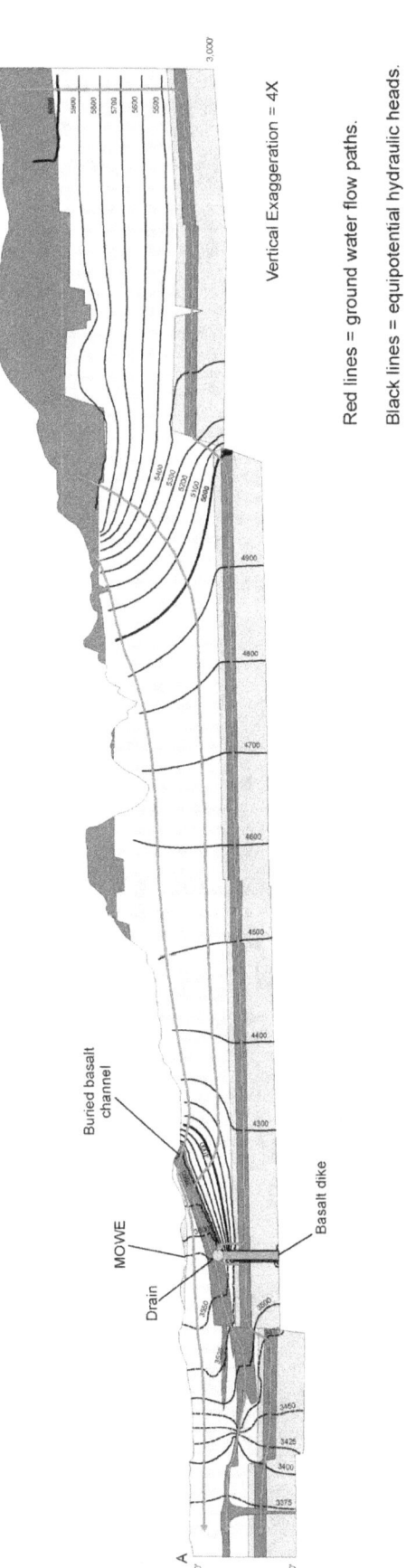

Vertical Exaggeration = 4X

Red lines = ground water flow paths.

Black lines = equipotential hydraulic heads.

Figure 53. Hydraulic heads and flow lines with basalt dike and drain.

61

Appendix 1. Original Water Sample Laboratory Data

Zip file online: Appendix 1 original water data.zip

Appendix 2. Original Rock Sample Laboratory Data

Zip file online: Appendix 2 original rock data.zip

Appendix 3. PHREEQC and NETPATH Files

Zip file online: Appendix 3 Inverse Modeling and Age Dating.zip

This file includes the following files:
    C-14 age date summary.xls
    CO2-C13 calcs.xls
And the following folders containing associated geochemical modeling files:
    Inverse Modeling and Age Dating
        MOWE-East-2008
        MOWE-Residence-2006
        MOW-West-118
        SODA-1
        SODA-C
    PHREEQC Saturation Indices

Note: When opened in WinZip, the files will appear in one general list, but upon extraction the files will be organized as listed above.

Appendix 4. Groundwater Flow Modeling Files

Zip file online: Appendix 4 Ground-water flow modeling.zip

This file includes a ReadMe file and the following folders containing associated flow modeling files:
    Simulation 1
    Simulation 2
    Simulation 3
    Simulation 4
    Source Codes

www.ingramcontent.com/pod-product-compliance
Lightning Source LLC
Chambersburg PA
CBHW080435290526
45791CB00008BA/2504